Book of Life

Consciousness for us to create a healing for
Heaven on a Paradise Earth

Written and Researched by Francess

In good faith

Fran

Also by Francess

(Formerly Frances Smith- Williams)

Healing Poems for Positive Love

Parousia – Love's Light

Parousia – Armageddon

Parousia - 12 Sonnets for God

Lost Loves

Ultimate Healing Poems - CD

Book of Life

Consciousness for us to create a healing for
Heaven on a Paradise Earth

Written and Researched by Francess

Book of Life

Consciousness for us to create a healing for
Heaven on a Paradise Earth

Written and Researched by Francess

Dedication

Dedicated to Everyone and Everybody: to all people from all nations, young old and all in between, to the animals and birds, reptiles and insects, the fish in the sea, the sea and the earth, the plant kingdom, the planet earth and the moon, the planets and universe. Dedicated to creating Positive Love in us here on Earth, worthy of honour and praise for Eden to return again for paradise here on Earth that is possible but dependent on our choices for Love and Peace. Let there be Positive Love for Positive Life. 'Let there be Light': Light in the world…. for you and for me, for us, for our children, for their children and for their children's children and so forth for an eternally peaceful future on our amazingly beautiful planet.

Acknowledgements

With thanks to The One God of Love made whole in us by His Love made manifest by causing His Love to become whole in us for Heaven and Peace on Earth and a healing for All Nations.

Thanks to His son, Jesus Christ: The Anointed One; the one anointed with the whole spirit of Love who teaches Love to become whole in us for fulfillment of the whole spirit of Love for happiness, joy, trust, security and peace on Earth.

Thanks to my family; to my families past, present and future.

Thanks to all my pets who sat with me through many years of work.

Thanks to all my friends and clients who have encouraged me over the years.

Thanks to Pauline Williams for art work on 'Cup of Love'.

Thanks to my life experience and learning that gave me the inspiration for this work, however I do believe prevention is better than cure and it is better not to need to be almost 'killed to make you stronger' and that we can attain to not hurting each other with sinful and selfish acts.

Thanks to Emma and Emma and her team, my patient printers and to Alan Roderick for help with edits and review.

Thanks to everyone who has helped in any way.

Thanks to God who is Love and Light for this beautiful world and creation of Love and Light made whole in us.

God's Love is always Positive.

The End is the Beginning, the Beginning is the End...

An Analysis of Positive Life through learning Positive Love for us to create Heaven on Earth for the Promised Land to come to be in accord with God's Promise to 'heal All Nations' for Peace and Love to prevail in man becoming kind in Love made whole with trust and security to sin and war no more.

$E=MC^2$ Albert Einstein applied to the cells in the body

Energy = Mass x the speed of Light which is the resonance of Love made Positive and whole for vibrant health and well being for Life.

It is our responsibility and choice.

2nd Timothy 3.

But know this, that in the last days critical times hard to deal with will be here. For men will be lovers of themselves, lovers of money, self assuming, haughty, blasphemers, disobedient to parents, unthankful, disloyal, having no natural affection, not open to any agreement, slanderers, without self control, fierce, without love of goodness, betrayers, headstrong, puffed up, lovers of pleasures rather than lovers of God, having a form of godly devotion but proving false to its power, and from these turn away…4:3 For there will be a period of time when they will not put up with the healthful teachings.

'Healthful teachings' God, God's Love is good for our psychological and emotional health and well being which is the positive energy that sustains our physical wellbeing by means of a positive mindset with Faith for Love and a healthy protective bio energy, the aura, the 'outer garments', or 'tent of God with mankind'. In my work I conclude God's Love is protecting the Love inside us by avoidance of stress which causes pain. God's Love creates natural endorphins in us for health and well being, it is why His teachings are worthy of total adherence and worship and honour in everyday life.
God's Love is the universal anti depressant.

Matthew 24:7 For nation will rise against nation and Kingdom against Kingdom and there will be food shortages and earthquakes in one place after another…22 In fact unless those days are cut short, no flesh would be saved., but on account of the chosen ones, those days will be cut short.

There will be many false Christ's and prophets – test every inspired expression. Test this work.

The End

The end is the start of the beginning of the word endorphin
the end of the quest for heart smiles in Love
mimicked by opium posing as opiates
killing pain knowing pleasure
addictive, seductive, seducing
ending enslavement to cortisols crying for an end,
the end; the release of endorphins
the dopamine, the serotonin, the oxytocin , the anandamide
binding the blood in marriage with Love
which is always positive
the endorphin is the end
the end is the beginning of The Word; Endorphin;
His Love in our blood
The beginning of freedom;
The end is the beginning of The Promise;
His Promise
The End is the beginning

'For look I am making all things new'.

Revelation 21:5

Love is not a cortisol.

The Lord's Prayer

Our Father, who art in Heaven

Hallowed be thy Name

Thy Kingdom Come

Thy Will be done on earth as it is in Heaven

Give us this day our daily bread

And forgive us our trespasses

As we forgive those who trespass against us

And lead us not into temptation

But deliver us from evil

For thine is the Kingdom

The power and the Glory

For ever and ever

Amen.

Psalm 48

1 JHVH (He who causes to become) is great and much to be praised in the city of our God, His Holy Mountain 2 Pretty for loftiness, the exultation of the whole earth, Is Mount Zion on the remote sides of the north, The town of the grand King. 3 In her dwelling towers God himself has become known as secure height. 4 For, Look! The Kings themselves have met by appointment, They have passed by together. 5 They themselves saw; so they were amazed. They got disturbed, they were sent running in panic. 6 Trembling itself took hold of them there, Birth pangs like those of a woman giving birth.
7 With an east wind you wreck the ships of Tar'shish. 8 Just as we have heard, so we have seen in the city of JHVH of armies, in the city of our God. God himself will firmly establish it to time indefinite. Se'lah. 9 We have pondered, O God, over your loving kindness In the midst of your temple. 10 Like your name, O God, so your praise is to the borders of the earth. Your right hand is full of righteousness itself. 11 May mount Zion rejoice. May the dependent towns of Judah be joyful on account of your judicial decisions. 12 March around Zion, YOU people, and go about it, Count its towers. 13 Set you hearts upon its rampart. Inspect its dwelling towers In order that you may recount it to the future generation. 14 For this God is our God to time indefinite, even forever. He himself will guide us until we die.

Jasper Judah Courage	Sapphire Reuben Faith	Chalcedony Gad Happiness	Emerald Asher Peace	Sardonyx Naphtali Wrestlings understand	Sardius Manasseh Forgive	Chrysolite Simeon Hear	Beryl Levi Adherence	Topaz Issachar Reward	Chrysoprase Zebulun Tolerance	Hyacinth Joseph Trust	Amethyst Ben Truth
Sapphire Reuben Faith	Chalcedony Gad Happiness	Emerald Asher Peace	Sardonyx Naphtali Wrestlings understand	Sardius Manasseh Forgive	Chrysolite Simeon Hear	Beryl Levi Adherence	Topaz Issachar Reward	Chrysoprase Zebulun Tolerance	Hyacinth Joseph Trust	Amethyst Ben Truth	Jasper Judah Courage
Chalcedony Gad Happiness	Emerald Asher Peace	Sardonyx Naphtali Wrestlings understand	Sardius Manasseh Forgive	Chrysolite Simeon Hear	Beryl Levi Adherence	Topaz Issachar Reward	Chrysoprase Zebulun Tolerance	Hyacinth Joseph Trust	Amethyst Ben Truth	Jasper Judah Courage	Sapphire Reuben Faith
Emerald Asher Peace	Sardonyx Naphtali Wrestlings understand	Sardius Manasseh Forgive	Chrysolite Simeon Hear	Beryl Levi Adherence	Topaz Issachar Reward	Chrysoprase Zebulun Tolerance	Hyacinth Joseph Trust	Amethyst Ben Truth	Jasper Judah Courage	Sapphire Reuben Faith	Chalcedony Gad Happiness
Sardonyx Naphtali Wrestlings understand	Sardius Manasseh Forgive	Chrysolite Simeon Hear	Beryl Levi Adherence	Topaz Issachar Reward	Chrysoprase Zebulun Tolerance	Hyacinth Joseph Trust	Amethyst Ben Truth	Jasper Judah Courage	Sapphire Reuben Faith	Chalcedony Gad Happiness	Emerald Asher Peace
Sardius Manasseh Forgive	Chrysolite Simeon Hear	Beryl Levi Adherence	Topaz Issachar Reward	Chrysoprase Zebulun Tolerance	Hyacinth Joseph Trust	Amethyst Ben Truth	Jasper Judah Courage	Sapphire Reuben Faith	Chalcedony Gad Happiness	Emerald Asher Peace	Sardonyx Naphtali Wrestlings understand
Chrysolite Simeon Hear	Beryl Levi Adherence	Topaz Issachar Reward	Chrysoprase Zebulun Tolerance	Hyacinth Joseph Trust	Amethyst Ben Truth	Jasper Judah Courage	Sapphire Reuben Faith	Chalcedony Gad Happiness	Emerald Asher Peace	Sardonyx Naphtali Wrestlings understand	Sardius Manasseh Forgive
Beryl Levi Adherence	Topaz Issachar Reward	Chrysoprase Zebulun Tolerance	Hyacinth Joseph Trust	Amethyst Ben Truth	Jasper Judah Courage	Sapphire Reuben Faith	Chalcedony Gad Happiness	Sardonyx Naphtali Wrestlings understand	Sardius Manasseh Forgive	Chrysolite Simeon Hear	Emerald Asher Peace
Topaz Issachar Reward	Chrysoprase Zebulun Tolerance	Hyacinth Joseph Trust	Amethyst Ben Truth	Jasper Judah Courage	Sapphire Reuben Faith	Chalcedony Gad Happiness	Emerald Asher Peace	Sardonyx Naphtali Wrestlings to understand	Sardius Manasseh Forgive	Chrysolite Simeon Hear	Beryl Levi Adherence
Chrysoprase Zebulun Tolerance	Hyacinth Joseph Trust	Amethyst Ben Truth	Jasper Judah Courage	Sapphire Reuben Faith	Chalcedony Gad Happiness	Emerald Asher Peace	Sardonyx Naphtali Wrestlings to understand	Sardius Manasseh Forgive	Chrysolite Simeon Hear	Beryl Levi Adherence	Topaz Issachar Reward
Hyacinth Joseph Trust	Amethyst Ben Truth	Jasper Judah Courage	Sapphire Reuben Faith	Chalcedony Gad Happiness	Emerald Asher Peace	Sardonyx Naphtali Wrestlings to understand	Sardius Manasseh Forgive	Chrysolite Simeon Hear	Beryl Levi Adherence	Topaz Issachar Reward	Chrysoprase Zebulun Tolerance
Amethyst Ben Truth	Jasper Judah Courage	Sapphire Reuben Faith	Chalcedony Gad Happiness	Emerald Asher Peace	Sardonyx Naphtali Wrestlings to understand	Sardius Manasseh Forgive	Chrysolite Simeon Hear	Beryl Levi Adherence	Topaz Issachar Reward	Chrysoprase Zebulun Tolerance	Hyacinth Joseph Trust

Contents

Prologue

Introduction   19

Chapter 1   23
Good Intention: Positive Love with Faith

Chapter 2   27
Fate or Choice: Discernment of Love or Fear

Chapter 3   30
All about the Cell: Creating Love or Fear

Chapter 4   37
East and West: Different ways of looking at the Body

Chapter 5   44
The Importance of the Insulin Factor to Stabilize our Blood

Chapter 6   46
The Blood: Another Potential to Stabilize our Bodies

Chapter 7   51
Time is Eternal: It is all about Perception

Chapter 8   55
The Life Cycle

Chapter 9   60
The Seven Spirits of Positive Love

Chapter 10   109
Israel or Is Real

Chapter 11   **129**
A New Jerusalem. Two Fold Peace. Peace Above and Peace
Below, Peace within ourselves and Peace with others; Heaven
on Earth

Chapter 12   **137**
The Significance of Twelve: 12

A Conclusion of How we work   **145**

Poem: A New Heaven: New Jerusalem Revelation 21   **162**

God's Healing Love   **163**

The Therapeutic Process for Healing Love   **164**

Scroll of Revelation 21: The Holy City: New Jerusalem: Zion
                                                                    166
A Vision of the Light: from Heaven to Earth   **168**

Some Poems   **170**

Notes and Reflections   **178**

Emotional Stress Processing Procedure   **180**

Notes   **187**

Resources and Bibliography   **190**

Author Biography   **204**

The End   **209**

Poppies

Floppy poppies floating in the sun
Are a source of joy for everyone
They should grow amongst the wheat we eat
And in small doses are a treat.

Like frankincense they conquer fear
But only if we respect them dear
They help remove the pain of man
But wont fulfil the challenge or plan.

You see it is up to us to grow
Like scarlet poppies in the snow
Fighting off the frost and cold with
Loves golden, reddened glow.

When we find that golden glow
Our own opiates we can grow.

Introduction

This book is about the concept of healthy mind and healthy body and how our thoughts, emotions and life experiences can affect our vitality and wellbeing. We have such an abundance of information on life style, exercise and diets, nutrition, medication, things that are good for us, things that are bad for us, so much so that it is totally confusing and often contradictory. Trends come and go. Too much knowledge can be very confusing and sometimes overwhelming with an uncertainty to what is right with no common sense. Cerebral knowledge can become more stressful than moderate accurate knowledge of what is right and beneficial, of knowledge that we can get a sense of and really embody into our lives. It is vitally important to our emotional wellbeing that we cultivate discerning positive thought patterns and behaviours that can lead us to health and happiness by developing all our senses fully.

What is often significant in every ailment is stress. Do you know what stress is? How can we define stress? And, what can we do about stress? What can you do about it? Can we control stress? Stress is unique for every individual depending on their interpretation of their life experiences. Stress is not always based in reality but stress always feels real. I hope to share ways of addressing principles of stress in order to help us relieve our stress and improve our energy and wellbeing.

This has the potential to help you to gain control of your health and wellbeing as an individual and show you the importance and usefulness of self-awareness as a way to help yourself.

The desire to heal is instinctive and healing has been a part of every culture and every era in man kind's history. The Egyptians, Romans, Jews, Chinese, Indians, Yogis, Buddhists, Muslims, Christians, Acupuncturists, Faith Healers, Massage Therapists, Reflexologists, Church Exorcists, Witch Doctors, Mayans and Aztecs and now modern medicine and surgery techniques. People from every part of the planet for all time have been seeking to help people remove pain and improve their health and wellbeing. There are countless remedies and traditions to help relieve and prevent illness that have been used for centuries and are now the basis of many modern pharmaceutical products. Generally it is in man's kind nature to want to help others to feel better and help each other if we can. Most mothers are inclined in this way and when their child hurts itself they will instinctively 'gently rub it better' as do both parents. However, natural touch has become not politically correct in these end days where touch has almost become limited to sexual with some trusts betrayed. Healthy touch is a very natural experience. I always say therapeutic massage is one of the best experiences in the world because it relaxes the body and mind and soothes aches and pains, it gives the 'feel good factor' which are endorphins in our blood and it has no negative side effects.

Positive Love is the conclusion form my study of scripture and healing (further definition in my book Healing Poems for Positive Love) can work for all removing the need for unhealthy competition with winners and losers for divided social structures thus creating a world that is equal, fair and just. Everyone has something to offer for the greater good of society and everyone is good at something when given the encouragement in their abilities and all are equally valuable.

For most people, every cell of the human body has all the information it needs to remain healthy in its DNA. This is in the language of chains and sequences of proteins. Problems can occur in the transporting of this genetic information from degeneration of telomeres, the tails of DNA information used to replicate at a cellular level. If the message, the genetic code has been damaged or deteriorated then problems will occur and aging, degeneration and dis-ease will result because the blueprint is damaged and incomplete.

The key to health and wellbeing is to minimize stress and toxins and optimize exercise and nutrition in a well-balanced way that allows for cells to be switched on and working optimally for life and creating energy and wellbeing. This is the feel good factor. But in order to perpetuate the feel good factor to last there is a need for *good morals* to prevail. Immorality is very seductive and physically gratifying temporarily, but psychologically and emotionally it is destructive because there is incongruence in the body and stress will prevail in this state of being. The body has an innate need for congruence, a need for truth to emerge for wholeness in mind and body where happiness, truth and openness can reside peacefully.

Our experience of life is totally down to what our cells are doing at every moment of every day. I hope and pray in time we will be able to see that we can all work together for good in the world for peace and Heaven on Earth.

In her book ' Switched On' Christine Houghton, a nutritional biochemist talks about this process and how important it is that the right detoxification messages are communicated through the cells for activating the elimination of toxins from the body in order to stay healthy and keep youthful.

Detoxification and a healthy digestive system are the basis of Naturopathic treatments and can be observed with Iridology in the eye. I also think that professional Kinesiology operates to reflect these processes.

We are what we eat and we are what we don't eliminate. Elimination of toxins from the body is a key part of health and wellbeing, like emptying the rubbish bin from our houses. We are also what we think and feel so discernment of emotional states of being is very relevant to our experience of life.

I hope this book will give you a new perspective to look at the human body and help you to learn some of the amazing powers of the human body to heal and repair given the right mindset, nutrients and environment. Perhaps it shows where science, faith, religion and consciousness can meet, all through the physiology of Love and Light for enlightenment of the healing power of Love and Light;

'Let there be Light'. 'Let Love conquer fear'.

'A healing for All Nations' Revelation 21:5

Chapter 1

Good Intention: Positive Love with Faith

Over two thousand years ago Hippocrates was a Doctor and teacher of medicine who realized the power of being able to help others. He realized the power to do good with good will and intention. Hippocrates was also aware of the corruption and vulnerability that could be exploited by a patient's vulnerability. The Hippocratic Oath is based on his philosophy of good intention to help someone in need. An oath that promotes honesty and integrity to the best of the practitioners ability. This is why modern day Doctors take the 'Hippocratic Oath' before they go into practice medicine. Good intention would be a positive model for everyone to live by and integrity is needed to create a basis of all good relationships. Hippocrates is credited with saying, "Let food be thy medicine and medicine be thy food." Living in the Mediterranean must have meant that Hippocrates could observe the effects of an abundance of good, healthy, fresh food had on people's health and wellbeing. I expect even then there was a clear distinction between the people living a clean, healthy life style and those who did not. Scientists are now backing up this intuitive knowledge and the properties of healthy organic foods are being proved with scientific knowledge. Natural organic methods are healthier than chemical enhanced growing.

Just over 2000 years ago Jesus Christ talked about ways for moral living in his Sermon on the Mount and said that "man should not live by bread alone" and spoke about the beatitudes for spiritual peace and happiness. Jesus said "Happy are those who mourn for they will be comforted" and as a therapist I know we have to mourn our hurts and pain to be free of the negative consequences they bring. The Sermon on the Mount included the Lord's Prayer which is a prayer about self-awareness, self-control and discernment for righteousness through accurate knowledge of right and wrong to bring about a better world for everyone with love.

Around two thousand years later in the late 1800s, Thomas Edison who invented the light bulb said;

"The doctor of the future would give no medicine, but will interest her or his patients in the care of the human frame, in a proper diet, and in the cause and prevention of disease."

Mahatma Gandhi said that "if the whole world lived by the standards from Jesus's Sermon on the Mount alone, that the world would be a better place." He also said that "Where there is love there is life." There are many wonderful quotes of wisdom for spiritual awareness for Positive Love and happiness to abound. (As found in abundance on social media now 2018).

From Aristotle BC to Jesus Christ AD and the Dalai Lama of today, all agree that the purpose of our life is to be happy through morality for Love and I believe this too. It is in our cells make up to find happiness and I think all the great teachings are leading us to happiness. Plato and Socrates, Jesus Christ and all the Prophets, Muhammad (pbuh)The Dalai Lama, Kant, to name a few with wisdom and discernment for love of life and good. There are many more in all forms of expression, art, poetry and writing, music, film in many walks of life. Our thoughts and actions and motives are as important as health and hygiene to us being happy and healthy. All true and faithful teachings attain to this love and peace.

Even though we have made some amazing progress in the medicine of today with medication, surgery, cleanliness and hygiene we are still suffering with degenerative diseases such as cancer, heart disease, diabetes, immune dis function, osteoporosis and painful arthritic diseases. Inflammation in the body causes great pain to many which is not always age related. Add to those the figures of depression and mental illness and those dependent on medications, I suggest we are missing a vital ingredient for our wellbeing.

In this book I will be looking at why and how living by raised spiritual and conscious standards of moral Love can alter and improve our quality of life today and why they are so important to mankind's wellbeing. I have found God's standards for Love through Faith are good for our health and well being. Everything is a choice.

Hippocratic Oath for World Peace

Inspired by Dylan Thomas's poem
'Do Not go Gentle into that Good Night'.

The World is filled with too much self loath
'rage, rage against the dying of the light'
shouldn't we all take the Hippocratic Oath?

'Not by bread alone' but give us our loaf
The Light has faded into a raging dark night
The World is filled with too much self loath.

World famine and greed, do you expect growth?
'do not go gentle into that good night'
shouldn't we all take the Hippocratic Oath?

People are starving and need a bread loaf
find joy, joy in the rising of The Light;
The World is filled with too much self loath.

Mix bread with les *oeuf* for some fine toast;
a golden dawn of new light that is bright,
shouldn't we all take the Hippocratic Oath?

'Do not go gentle' into that dark night like most,
but find rapture for the coming of The Light
The World is filled with too much self loath,
We must all take the Hippocratic Oath.

Amen, Ameen, Shalom, Namaste, Peace to all.

Chapter 2

Fate or Choice: Discernment of Love or Fear

Why will some people catch a bug and others not? Why are some people phobic about spiders and others about heights? Why do some people look younger than their age and others look much older?

How we experience life is all to do with how the body processes at a cellular level. This is a combination of what we have inherited in our genes and what we have experienced in our lives. What we have done with our lives and how we see things in life.

Half empty and half full are two very different places to base your thoughts. Genetic inheritance "it runs in the family, my mum had it, my dad had it". Sometimes this is true, but not always. Is an ailment because of a lifestyle choice, or is the ailment a nutritional or psychological deficiency? If a parent has a nutritional deficiency then their child could have the same deficiency because their lifestyle and dietary choices are similar and not supplying the nourishment needed for the body function to occur. But it can also be the child does not inherit anything, why may this be? Some hereditary traits can be overcome with lifestyle and nutrition, and in my experience also with thoughts.

Nutrition is like having the right fuel in your tank. A petrol engine will not run on diesel. Different body functions require different nutrients and if the fuel isn't there then it isn't going to happen. As we learn more about the way the body functions as a whole and the individual properties of nutrients which science is revealing then we can design and tailor exactly to our bodies needs. This is already done with Kinesiology muscle testing and even some hereditary traits can sometimes be resolved.

With life style choices and care of ourselves we can assert self-control for a healthy life with autonomy by self-awareness and self knowing.

Everything depends on our choices and discernment and whether something is positively upbuilding to our whole health and wellbeing of mind, body and spirit, or not.

Adam, Eve and St Agnes Genesis 2: 17 'to positively die'

('neither will they learn war no more') Isaiah 2:4

Oh! what if St Agnes had been in the Garden of Eden
on that fateful day, could we be living in paradise now?
Would we be living in paradise now?
Perhaps, just, maybe...

Could we be positively living with no hurts or pain?
Just love and kindness
No jealousy, no crime, no sickness, no shame

No death of Love, no death of the Positive Spirit, no death of joy
No wars - just 'wonderful counsel': no wars - just 'Princely peace'
No wars - an 'eternal parent guiding'

What is the point of fighting? All for the same thing anyway;
that elusive prize of Positive Life; peace and love for our loved ones

'Do beat your swords into plowshares and your spears into pruning
shears' as it is written (Isaiah)

Go grow your own paradise and your own food
grow your own herbs and your own flowers,
learn grace for self control, autonomy and self worth,
heal and grow in Positive Spirit

Love each other as yourself, Love your neighbour and be kind
give love freely as   Love   takes   time.

Strong,   yet fragile;   Sacred

One betrayal will burst Love's bubble.
We become negative and fearful; not able to trust
so never betray and we can Positively Live now.

Oh St Agnes, where were you that fateful day
when mankind Positively Died?

Chapter 3

All about the Cell: Creating Love or Fear

Sometimes the most complicated things are really very simple. The human body appears very complicated but actually runs on some simple moral guidelines. If we follow those healthy guidelines the body looks after itself. The body can look after itself. Is that surprising to you? The human body grows and does complicated functions every moment of every day and we don't even think about them. Often the body is totally taken for granted until something starts to go wrong or hurt. We only think about our head if we have a head ache. This is simple because the principles that keep us happy and healthy also keep our cells happy and healthy. If our cells are happy and healthy then life works, energy is created, toxins are eliminated and nutrients are utilized for body functions, regeneration and elimination, building new cells and energy. We should be doing the same things on all levels, physical, mental and emotional, taking in, absorbing, sorting, utilizing and eliminating. This is the process of all living organisms and systems, this is the process of a cell and this is the process of life.

The cell has a format. It is a single cell with coded gateways in and out of the cell skin which is called the cell membrane. This allows the flow of blood, water, oxygen, nutrients and molecules in and out of the cell. The cell membrane has the appearance of a mountain range which greatly increases its surface area.

The cell membrane contains the cytoplasm which is the fluid containing the cell nucleus which contains the genetic information in the DNA required for making new cells, the blueprint for making you and me, us. The mitochondria are organelles which produce energy; think of them like the powerhouses. They act like a digestive system taking in nutrients and breaking them down for energy. This is called cell respiration and happens where oxygen interacts with the proteins and water in the cell to digest and produce energy. Mitochondria are unusual because they have two membranes, the inner one folded many times to increase surface area optimizing function. This folded structure is also seen in our brains. Different cells have different requirements for mitochondria depending on the type of cell. A muscle cell will have lots and the cells can even grow, move and combine with other mitochondria depending on the energy requirements. (www.biology4kids.com).

The mRNA is the messenger which takes the instructions from the DNA in the nucleus of the cell to the cell cytoplasm where the instructions are carried out by the cell organelles.

We are made up of trillions of microscopic cells which are self contained and self regulating individuals working together for the greater good of the body that they are. The cells are happy just being, doing what they are designed to do and in a positive, healthy, nourishing environment they will thrive. Would our society be better off if we mirrored our cells? All working together for the greater good. Should we, could we, can we as a species mirror our cells ability to work together harmoniously? Could we work together for unity and community, oneness? Can we work for the greater good like our cells do? Where we are all equally valuable in our positive contributions.

If the environment is not positive, healthy and nourishing the cells will not thrive. They will struggle to survive and not be able to attain to optimum states of health. As within so without. Our cells, ourselves and our environment are ultimately all the same processes in action. Indeed so is the universe as it absorbs imploding stars and gives birth to new stars and suns for light and dark to be separated.

The cells determine us, they create us. They have the ability to create a wonderful, joyous healthy body. A body that resides in the Para Sympathetic Nervous System where Positive Love creates endorphins and feelings of security, trust, love, happiness and wellbeing.

Contrary to the Para-Sympathetic Nervous System is the Sympathetic Nervous System which is activated by the state of fear or stress. The cells produce adrenalins and cortisols in order to super charge the body out of the dangerous environment, real or perceived.

This is often viewed as a primitive reflex but it is so much more than primitive. I would go as far as say the very way the Autonomic Nervous System works is towards creating the perfect environment for us to live happily, for the cells to flourish and create life for us to enjoy and embody. The primitive reflex activates the reptilian brain and limbic system for adrenaline surged high physical performance away from danger but it also shuts down the frontal brain of emotional processing and reason. In its simplicity it is very complex and in its complexity it is very simple. We are truly wonderfully and perfectly created by some form of intelligence way beyond our capabilities. Fear and stress bring pain and conflict, disease whilst reason and a positive state of love bring comfort, harmony, wellbeing and peace. Our sufferings can really teach us to change our ways if we listen.

****

A completely independent structure working in harmony with others. And honouring The DNA's precise instructions for making proteins and maintaining health. What is apparent is the DNA is giving the genetic coding via the mRNA to be processed by the organelles. The DNA is set and is unchangeable, the blueprint for reproduction.

It is interesting to view this as the same pattern as God of Love as the blue print for Love, The DNA of Love and Jesus Christ – the whole spirit of Love giving the instructions
of Love who is God for Love to become in us is like the mRNA delivering the message for coding Love in us.

The outcome is a result of the accuracy of messages received and processed and the response of the body/cell to environment and situation based on previous learning experience and degrees of what is a right response and ultimately on accurate knowledge.

Ultimately the cell will produce body biochemical for the states of love or fear emotionally, psychologically and physiologically.

E.g. we may have a fear of something based on our experiences in life, for example commitment. With a fear of commitment it is very hard to sustain a relationship and generally what many would like is stable relationships. However, if our body responds with the stress response of fear then this take us away from the very thing we want and the resulting behaviours destroy the relationship you have. Yet in truth, the behavior that sets up the negative reaction was wrong, not right, not Positively Loving to create safety or trust for peace and security for Love to reside in our bodies. Basically trust is lost and replaced by fear and anxiety resulting in stress and anxieties and fleshly responses as defined in Galatians 5:19 which are basically hormonal imbalances created from stress hormones. Therefore when trust is needed the body bio chemicals like oxytocin have not been created learned. This can be learned or relearned with conscious effort and understanding and behaviours relearned for awareness and healing.

Is the cell working independently of brain signals or are the chemical messengers produced by the cell influencing the brains emotional responses? Or is the brain dictating responses or are the two working together simultaneously? Are they designed to work together?

The fleshly experience gives messages but the brain must evaluate and consciously choose the response. Likewise with intention we can choose and dictate the fleshly experience.

The best response for an all positive outcome is based on the accurate knowledge of Positive Love and truth in the body and applied to override negative learning experiences.

Fear and mistrust are the result of negative experiences based on the inaccurate knowledge of mans reactions without accurate knowledge for creating Positive Love and truth.

Accurate knowledge of self-control in Positive Love in the Para Sympathetic Nervous System does know best, this is where we find reason.

In stress we are a fear based survival mechanism reacting in a fire fighting response with little idea of true and honest Positive Love.

Only with Positivity through Positive Love in the Para Sympathetic Nervous System can mankind actively practice true and honest love and gain trust and security for everyone.

Could and should our brains be more balanced, more discerning, more connected? Does consideration of Positive Love values in our lives increase our wellbeing, vitality and our health? Can conscious understanding of these help guide us for cultivating love over fear?

We can influence these states of being from our behaviours, our belief systems and our consciousness and self-control of our emotions. We have the power to empower ourselves for Positive Love for Positive Life if we choose to.

Or we can be out of self-control responding to fear based messages of insecurity causing chaos and conflict. We have the power of choice. We know inside what is right and what is not right, haram or halal and we can feel the difference of love or fear, right or wrong and which are our sources of motivation?

Everything is a choice, we have the choice by discernment.

Our Amazing Bodies

(Inspired by Galatians 5:19-22)

I love bodies living and actualising dreams
self evolving for self knowledge to express
ourselves creatively for life;

Not just clumps of meat
Not just clumps of cells
Not just physiological functions;

Not just anatomical structures
with complex Latin names

Complex they are,
Complex we are
Only flesh we are not.

Chapter 4

East and West: Different ways of looking at the Body

Kinesiologists muscle test the body by monitoring muscle responses to various stimuli. I have been asked countless times what are you testing? Who are you talking too? Where are the responses coming from? Are you dowsing? Is it dowsing? Is it divination? Is it good? What exactly are we testing? Sometimes a muscle fix can be so instantaneous it is almost miraculous and mind blowing to a persons thinking parameter. However I think this is the miracle of our bodies intelligence and capability to heal in accord with how we have been designed, created and made; all glory to something far greater than a human being for this.

A muscle test is monitor of a muscle response in accord with its ability to produce energy. Muscle testing assesses the flow of energy in the meridian flow, the electromagnetic flow of the body which related to specific muscles and these are determined by the nervous system and organ function. We do not make any diagnosis but measure the muscle response of strong or weak to specific stimuli. There are machines now that can identify these responses.

I started to analyze my findings in relation to the human body in it's biochemical structure and emotional state of being and added the psychological known and repressed patterns of love or fear. I had certain guidelines and principles I used for this.

I have studied this extensively by observing the body responses and furthering my anatomical and physiological studies as well as in my own life issues.

I also studied The Bible teachings and Holy Scriptures to study why Jesus Christ was and is the most renowned healer of all time. Most people know about Jesus and what he did for people, but how many recognize what he really did as a healer? I studied the Holy Scriptures not as a religion but as a psychological concept for health and wellbeing in relation to what I know about the principles of healing. There are many who follow health gurus and models but I wanted to find something complete, more whole. I also wanted to find why Jesus Christ was and is the greatest and most renowned healer of all time. I also wanted to give him the recognition for this.

I studied beauty and massage therapies, energetic medicine and naturopathic principles, nutrition, yoga and eastern philosophies, new age etc., anatomy and physiology, counselling, touched on psychology and philosophy and anything I could for health, happiness and wellbeing.

When I married together my knowledge with the teachings of Jesus Christ I could then understand the meaning and value of The Bible as a book for creating health and happiness in us by means of teaching us how to love in a positive and truthful way. Many of the principles of the teachings are found in other doctrines as well.

My findings revealed to me that the scriptural teachings are about how to regulate and stabilize our body through the practice of Positive Love created by our thoughts, our behaviours, our intentions and our actions, out thoughts, words and deeds, our mind, body and spirit.

I think the majority of people know the message of The Holy scriptures but not in their entirety for the promise of heaven and peace on earth and the promise of every tear and all pain being wiped away by God's Love made whole as written in The Book of Revelation. The celebration of Jesus as a baby being born at Christmas and dying on the cross at Easter dominate the church annual celebrations and there are glimpses of the promised land and acts of Christ and his apostles in between. However I think there is so much more to know and understand. I think the way Jesus acted and thought and the principles of spiritual concepts are all about principles of healing and energy knowledge that lead us to happiness and fulfillment in our lives that embrace all life forms. If we read the bible with understanding of energy and light and quantum physics the teachings make perfect sense for healing through Love made whole, the meaning of the very name of Jesus Christ.

My findings reveal that the psychology of faith in a God of Love is good for us, is good for our health and well being by cultivating Positive Love through the power of reason and rejecting and overcoming negativity, stress and fear. This is universal across all positive teaching of self-awareness and self-control for the greater good of all mankind and all life forms and the environment and planet. Please note this is not specific to any one religious order but is all encompassing of whole and fulfilling writings for attaining to Oneness through Love made whole in us for peace and unity and well being.

I think this occurs in the body by the Autonomic Nervous System which determines whether we live in love or fear, stress or the positive state of love by the mechanisms in the body that connect to the cells to produce adrenaline or endorphins, stress and fear or love.

By this measure we can attain self-control of ourselves, our bodies and minds and determine how we live in accord with spirit or flesh – as defined at Galatians 5: 19 -22.

This also is what gives us free will by choice. We make choices that determine who and what we are.

These choices determine how we feel in ourselves and then determine what choices we make to determine our next choice. Healthy choices create healthy choices. Not healthy choices create more unhealthy choices. The more unhealthy the choice, the more stimulants are needed to regain energy – even if falsely stimulated which result in addictions.

Our choices create empowerment and control over ourselves; Discernment – right or wrong, healthy or unhealthy, haram or halal, the blessings or curse. Everything is our choice.

We need to choose to remain in our Para Sympathetic Nervous system for Positive Life which means we need to avoid stress and fear which creates negativity and fear in the Sympathetic Nervous System. We need to avoid stress or fear in mind, body and spirit to know no bad – the tree of the knowledge of good and bad? We can know bad and entertain with bad but what effect does it have on a person, on their cells and how they live their life? We know all these things yet so many still choose the 'wrong' things and then wonder why they have problems and want those problems to be fixed when perhaps a recommended prevention would have been a wiser choice. We can choose anything, but not all things are healthy or wholesome or up building for love and health.

Acupuncture and Energetic Medicine are aware of the need for flow in the body and work to clear blocks in the flow of energy by stimulating the acupuncture points which are closely linked with the nerves and messaging systems between the body and brain.   The concept of relaxation through touch and smell are the basis of many body treatments such as Aromatherapy and Reflexology and

Massage Techniques. Reversal Therapy, Emotional Freedom Technique Hypnotherapy and Neuro Linguistic Programming and Counselling and Psychotherapy, Psychiatry, Cognitive Behavioral Therapies.   These all work with the mind to overcome negative fearful states of being with Positive thoughts and realization through reason and conscious awareness. There are countless methods that are beneficial to all encompassing all for Positive good. The abundance of spas has raised the awareness of the feel good factor of treatments and relaxation and the benefits of touch. It is a misconception of western society that touch is mainly for sex and this is destructive to shows of genuine affection between genuine people. Some people don't like touch and to some people touch has associated connotations that are not always positive. Of course physical love between lovers is physical, mental and emotional with touch and is the pinnacle of union with another being which enters the spiritual realms of consciousness and should be honored, valued and sacred, hence marriage.   Are we not all really seeking peace, happiness and contentment in life? By utilizing all our senses we can attain to this. We need to be sensitive, sensitive to others and ourselves, we need to be sensible by discernment and to come to our senses to live fully. Let us embrace our senses for all humanity. I see desensitization to feelings and morals in our society at the moment which is not creating stability in any way. In fact we are seeing instability of mental health in all ages now more than ever.

Historically in medicine, contrary to the ancient Eastern methods of working with subtle energy in the body the west took the path of looking inside the body by anatomical dissection.

There would have been knowledge of the flesh from wounds and wars for all time and with animals being used for food, so there would have been knowledge of the inside of the body and it's flesh. The first main documenting of the anatomy of the flesh was done by Claudius Galen, a physician, writer and philosopher to the Roman Empire who worked extensively on stitching and repairing the Gladiators wounds. His dissections and writings were mainly of animals as it was an offence to dissect humans at that time. His observations and writings were used for more than a thousand years. Galen was then challenged by a Belgian Anatomist Andreas Vesalius whose book on the Structure of the Human Body – 'De Humani Corporis Fabrica' presented detailed fine drawings that were the origin of anatomical detail obtained by dissection.

Perhaps with the onset of spiritual concepts and teachings of the Roman Catholic Church where Jesus' teachings merged with the Roman and Pagan celebrations and the teaching of the immortality of the soul, heaven and hell, purgatory and redemption. Perhaps the early anatomists were looking inside the body for evidence of the soul. Originally the anatomical dissections were performed on criminals after execution, could they have been looking for the evil spirits inside that caused the wrong to be done?

By examining the physical body, what it is made up of and how it works, (anatomy and physiology) has led us to amazing progress in medicine and science and is the origin of surgery. When we put energy medicine with orthodox medicine we have a complete model for prevention and repair of almost every ailment. Awareness of the body also overcomes the initial fear and repulsion which comes initially from seeing what we are really made up of, muscles, bones, nerves, and organs etc. which are all made up of countless individual cells.

As we understand how we work more and more we have empowerment for self-control over ourselves.

With these two models of medicine we have the ability to look after and keep our minds and bodies healthy and happy, energized by positive vibration of Positive Love, trust and faith. How conscious we are becoming of the way life works in us.

We now need to understand how to create that positive energy of health and vitality and the positive thought patterns and behaviours that lead to cultivating a positive happy life with love. We know the difference between right and wrong, halal and haram and some have just gone off track in the name of selfish pleasures and self gain. We need to get back to community and individual identity and accountability for recognition of each other in order to find positive life working for everyone which in turn allows personal relationships to thrive for families to be born and children to have security and protection for continuum of our species with Love in accord with Love made positive and whole.

2nd Timothy – after describing the state of unkind beings in the last days says 'there is a time they will not put up with the healthful teachings'.

Chapter 5

The Importance of the Insulin Factor to Stabilize Our Blood

When we enter stress and fear our digestive system is closed down and the blood sugar level is raised by an influx of stress hormones like adrenaline and the cortisols to raise glucose into the blood stream. This powers our brain to function quickly to get us out of danger by powering the body to action. This is a temporary physiological state and as the body responds to the sugar high by increasing insulin then the body will desire to slow down, sleep and recuperate. This is the process the body will go through every time the adrenalines or blood sugars are raised. The result is ebbs and flows of energy which when extreme can become diabetic tendencies with a loss of this control mechanism.

If we can remain in a state of Positive Love in the body by being in the Para Sympathetic Nervous System then the digestion works optimally and blood sugars do not fluctuate so much and we remain physiological stabilized biochemically.

To remain physiologically stabilized means we have to fuel our bodies regularly with good wholesome nutrition, we have to have positive thoughts and emotions and we have to act in accordance with others wellbeing in a truly altruistic way.

This is easy when we know how but there are many unconscious causes of stress which jeopardize this function.
The catch in this is that adrenaline produces elated feelings of invincibility that are addictive. The heightened state of awareness and strength become dependent on stimulants like caffeine and other forms of drugs that will create stress in the body by means of producing adrenaline. The modern business world is powered by adrenaline.

****

This also gives a change in the experience of time as time is short while the adrenalin is pumping and we need to remove ourselves from that danger before it runs out. Hence the stress in the world, in the work place is always rushing to deadlines and trying to be the fastest and the best, the first primarily driven by money. Do we really need to compete when we could all work together for the greater good and improve life for everyone not motivated by money but by a raised standard of living for all. This would be working accord with the spirit of Love which is worthy of honour.

Stressed people never have time. Working mothers are always rushing and short on time because there is just physically too much to do in a day. Yes we can do it and are doing it but where is the quality time on a daily basis with our children and families. Everyone feels the stress. Does it really need to be like this? We all need a work life balance that keeps us in Positive Love without stress to be in a positive spirit of happiness and security. Surely there are many positive solutions to all these stressors. Time is actually eternal and we should have all the time in the world. It is our man made constraints that create the constraints, cages and boundaries. See more in chapter 7.

Chapter 6

The Blood, Another Potential to Stabilize Our Bodies

All of this is determined by the chemical composition of the blood, the hormone levels and blood sugars. The Bible says we should attain to the Blood of Christ. Christ's blood must have been abundant with endorphins created by embodying Positive Love without fear. The Blood of Christ. If we translate the meaning of the name Jesus Christ, it means anointed with Gods spirit of love. A whole Spirit. Holy Spirit from God. Jesus entered into heaven by his blood. Could he have attained to this by creating the right body biochemistry for love by manifesting the emotional and psychological states of

Love

Faith

Discernment

Righteousness

Consciousness

Brotherly Love

Unity for Communion with Love for

Peace

'Love God and others as self' for Peace with others and self for

'The peace of God that excels all thought' Philipians 4:7

The peace of confidence in Positive Love made whole in us for fruits of the spirit to become abound namely Love, Joy, Faith, Mildness, Goodness, Kindness with Patience and Self Control not to sin for Peace within the self and with others in accord with The Golden Rule to Love God who is Love which is always positively up building, to Love others *as* self. For peace to come to be there has to be quiet conscience not activated by the fear stress response to fears or guilt and shame.

Peace, contentment, happiness and calmness. Mildness, forgiving, patient and kind. Loving, caring, helping, hoping and sharing. These are all positive emotional states of being. Positive body bio chemicals in the blood, made in the blood, determined by the blood. Neuro chemicals and hormones determine how we feel, they affect how we feel.

How we feel affects how we relate to others. To be truly altruistic we need to feel good and free of hurts and pains to be energized for Positive Life.

To be free of emotional pain we need to find forgiveness and forgiveness requires repentance and learning with understanding and compassion. True repentance allows for forgiveness which allows for trust and realization and flow of friendship, relationships and interactions.

No repentance indicates there is no sensitivity or consciousness of another person's feelings. This makes it difficult to find reason and understanding allowing for conscious realization and forgiveness. The only way to peace is in each individual. Each individual has to attain to this peace only with the belief in wholeness, oneness in love and in faith, there is no other way.

Love that is positive is Love; The One who causes (love) to become, The One that creates, The One that is what He is: Love. All this has been written already. We just need to get back to the understanding of what it means for life.

When we are in positive states of being our whole body bio chemistry changes. This can be determined by our intentions and behaviours and by the blood chemistry. It is faith and trust versus stress and fear, endorphins versus adrenaline, good versus bad, love versus fear. Science has now identified many of these components in the blood.
Body Bio chemicals such As Glutamic Acid/ Glutamate, Leptin, Neuropeptide Y, Anandamide, Complement Factors, Erythropoietin Epo, Glucagon-Like Peptide 1 Glp1, Glutathione Peroxidase, Nociceptin/ Orphanin Fq2, Phosphatidyl-Inositol, Superoxide Dismuase/ Sod Ubiquitin Apf-1, Carbonic Anhydrase, Fibrinogen, Glycogen, Leucine Enkephalin, Methionine Enkephalin, Neuromedin B, 2-Phenylethylamine Pea/B-Phenethylamine, Purine, Serine. Body bio chemicals such as serotonin, oxytocin and endorphins.

These body bio chemicals work in the body for 'the feel good factor' and relief of pain. Pain is primarily emotional and held in the body by stress which causes blocks and denials of truths. Healing pain comes from acknowledging the truths and finding understandings and reasoning them out within the benchmark of Love being made positive again, consciousness for making the spirit of Love whole again through righteousness.

Anandamide is the bliss molecule and like steps to heaven can only be attained to when the moral codes of conduct of and in Love have been attained to in thought, word and deed and only with the positive psychology of Love through Faith. Stress and doubt and fear will block this state of being and the physiology cannot be reached.

This is how we can attain to rapture and bliss in Love in us which I propose is the Heaven on Earth promised by God and only attainable though the whole spirit of Love embodied in us. The meaning of the name of His Son and all sons and daughters to be. This I believe is faithful and true and what the pattern of The Holy City, The New Jerusalem reveals.

The End   Revelation 21:5

The end is the start of the beginning of the word endorphin
the end of the quest for heart smiles in Love
mimicked by opium posing as opiates
killing pain knowing pleasure
addictive, seductive, seducing
ending enslavement to cortisols crying for an end,
the end; the release of endorphins
the dopamine, the serotonin, the oxytocin , the anandamide
binding the blood in marriage with Love
which is always positive
the endorphin is the end
the end is the beginning of The Word; Endorphin;
His Love in our blood
The beginning of freedom;
The end is the beginning of The Promise;
His Promise
The End is the beginning
For 'look I am making all things new'.

Love is not a cortisol.

Chapter 7

Time is Eternal: It is all about Perception

Time is a totally relative manmade concept. Is there really little or no time? Time is eternal isn't it? In the Parasympathetic Nervous System there is time, time is eternal and things will come to be when they come to be. There is no need to rush. Everything will be fine, everything will be perfect and on time.

Stress and fear with no faith means that time is finite and will run out. Man thinks of time as linear with mortality, death at its end. The perspective of life beginning as a baby growing up becoming a child, teenager, adult leading on to aging and becoming old and death is a timeline of life. However is this true, is it fact and docs it need to be like this?

I think time can be viewed differently. I propose time can be viewed and measured emotionally, psychologically by completeness and wholeness of tasks and spirit. When we can give birth to something, create it, complete it, finish and make perfect, make whole then feelings of achievement, contentment, confidence, wholeness, completeness will arise. These in turn create positive energy in us which energizes and enthuses our very being resulting in fulfillment, happiness, faith and confidence. A project becomes complete, should be appreciated and enjoyed, celebrated and then the next one can begin.

Time as a whole O not as linear ---.

These in turn gives confidence and happiness and fulfillment. It doesn't matter what stage of life. whether it is a baby learning to crawl or walk, a child painting a picture, an adult painting a picture, an artist painting a picture, a child looking after its pet, a farmer tending to his animals, a zoo keeper looking after his animals, a mother or father or young adult cooking dinner, setting the table or parents creating and enterprising business, nurses looking after patients, doctors prescribing medicine, cleaners polishing the ward, looking after the home, the list is endless.

It is by the completion of creations that we find fulfillment. By a doctor helping someone to get better, by a dustman removing our rubbish, by a dentist removing the tooth that is aching, by the assistant cleaning the instruments, by a teacher imparting knowledge to activate the pupils learning and seeing where they then go with it, by the cooks cooking school dinners, by the surgeons operating to save a life and by the nurses follow up care, by performers entertaining and audience, by the audience seeing the whole show to the end, by musicians playing music and by learning to play a musical instrument. We all need each other's help and who is really the greatest and most valuable? Are we not all needed and therefore of equal value? Fulfillment of being pleasant and interested in the people you serve if you work in a shop or restaurant or in the public service industries. Time is a great gift. Time can work as an emotional and psychological process for fulfillment.

Man puts value on time that is endless. Like money, whatever the benchmark of value it only gets raised. Are we reaching a point where we don't have time to talk to each other, where our time is all too valuable to give freely? This is a worrying thought. Why not reset the benchmark? Time values are relative.

The only place in time we can really make change is in the now, in the present.

Presence

Today is our present
and it is a present
only if and when we are present
and it should be pleasant,
Life is His gift.

Chapter 8

The Life Cycle

The Life Cycle for creating Positive Love, Trust and Security for Peace within and Peace without.

The Corpus Callosum is a part of the brain which joins right and left hemispheres of the brain for whole brain integration and enlightenment and understanding. In the physiological state of stress and fear this connection is cut off and not able to function. The power of love and reason with faith. The Corpus Callosum allows for whole brain integration and function. Could this be the way enlightenment?

Corpus Callosum

Positive Love+	- Negative Fear
Para Sympathetic	Sympathetic
Endorphins	Adrenaline
Love	Fear
Forebrain	Reptilian brain
Reason	Stress
Rational	Irrational
Fruits of the spirit	Traits of the flesh
Peace	Conflict
Yin	Yang

This is based on my knowledge of the physical and energetic body, mental and emotional states of being and the stress response, The Holy Scriptures teachings of love, Yoga traditions, meditation, healing, chakras, meridians, brain science and life.

When we are in stress and fear then the corpus callosum does not connect the brain hemispheres for complete rational thinking and reason. When the corpus callosum is functioning then both hemisphere of the brain can be utilized to allow for complete processing of ideas and enlightenment. The corpus callosum is activated by the Parasympathetic Nervous System and positive neuro-chemicals and needs the knowledge of these emotional and psychological states of being. It is only when we have the higher and harder to attain to more humble emotional states of grace, gratitude, appreciation, forgiveness and repentance, being able to say sorry, realize a mistake has been made and be able to put right that the brain can activate all areas for enlightened consciousness, self actualization for healing to occur. A dying away to the ego also known as the nafs.

In energy flows of the body this is represented by the flow of what we call 8s. By tracing 8s and infinites over the body as a whole or over specific areas and cells or by drawing them on paper there seems to be an integration of left and right brain functions that can help facilitate learning. This has been utilized in Kinesiology techniques for some time to help with learning disabilities and dyslexia conditions as well has restoring balance to the body for well being.

I think they also can be looked at helping the communication between two on all levels. It is as if two isolated individuals become one integrated being with two parts. Think of opening up whole brain function, think of two cells opening up communication and interaction, think of two people becoming united by shared thoughts and feelings, think of two lovers becoming one. It is the conscious engagement that gives rise to the communication.

Could this be the elusive Holy Grail? The Cup of Love, and I say Positive Love because there are different forms of love.

In the west there is a great misconception that touch is primarily sexually orientated and that sex equates love. I think these areas need far more reasoning on the healthy benefits of natural touch, connection and healing for healthy connections to one another.

The Cup of Positive Love represents positive, connected , compassionate relationships between people and all living beings. The communication and unity of thought? The communion of ideals, oneness of spirit, oneness in energy that is Positive and like attracting like? Positive friendships and relationships and with each other.

The Life Cycle

The End   Revelation 21:5

The end is the start of the beginning of the word endorphin
the end of the quest for heart smiles in Love
mimicked by opium posing as opiates
killing pain knowing pleasure
addictive, seductive, seducing
ending enslavement to cortisols crying for an end,
the end; the release of endorphins
the dopamine, the serotonin, the oxytocin , the anandamide
binding the blood in marriage with Love
which is always positive
the endorphin is the end
the end is the beginning of The Word; Endorphin;
His Love in our blood
The beginning of freedom;
The end is the beginning of The Promise;
His Promise
The End is the beginning
For 'look I am making all things new'.

'Love is not a cortisol.'

Chapter 9

The Seven Spirits of Positive Love

The Cup of Positive Love

The scriptures say God is Love and God is Light so I am asking is Love God? And is Light God? And what are Love and Light and how do they manifest in us. If God is something we worship and attain to be like then Positive Love is certainly worthy of this because it creates peace and harmony among everyone within and without. Should we all be seeking Positive Love for happiness and peace? Light is preferable to dark because we can see but Light is also warmth and energy. When we have energy and vitality we have Love and Joy in accord with fruits of the spirit and we are 'zinging' (as one of my Health Kinesiology instructors says). We smile, we laugh, we share, we make music and dance and express ourselves just for the sheer pleasure of life and being able to express ourselves without fearful inhibitions (and without the need for drugs or alcohol in order to do so). We make merry and happy. This is Positive Love in action and is the place where we can be together in harmony. The place where we can share, eat and drink, dance, talk, create music and wholesome entertainment and celebrate together to celebrate the joy of life with thanks and praise to God, through Jesus' name; through being anointed with the whole spirit of Love made whole in us for the fruits of the spirit to be made manifest in us.

From my study of Energy, Anatomy & Physiology, Medicine, Healing, and The Holy Scriptures I propose that The Book of Revelation reveals the Cup of Love, perhaps even the Holy Grail. The seven spirits here have been discerned from chapters 2 and 3 and are in accord with all the whole teachings of Love made whole.

The cup of Positive Love is the about the ability to relate peacefully with other people and contains 'the 7 spirits of God', or seven psychological and emotional thought processes we need to know to attain to Love and Light to be made whole in us. These seven spirits fit with the healing properties of the gemstones cited in Revelation 21 and the names of the sons of Israel also cited as part of The Holy City which reveal the consciousness of making Love whole and complete in us and also the consciousness the apostles must have attained to having learned from Jesus directly.

From my research these states of being are:

Love

Faith

Discernment

Righteousness

Consciousness

Brotherly Love/ Friendship

Communion/ Unity/ Oneness

(as depicted on the image cover on the front of this book which I commissioned to be painted by Pauline Williams.)

Resulting in unity, peace, joy, happiness and health and wellbeing, vitality and energy.

These are the psychological and emotional states that power our very being, they power our cells, they power our organs and they empower our lives. They operate in us at the speed of light, they are instantaneously creating energy, light and consciousness at quantum levels.

This is also the qualities of energy in our bodies known as the Radiant Circuits or Extra ordinary Channels or the Strange Flows from ancient knowledge of the acupuncture meridians which really allow us to experience the joy of positive emotional spirit in life. Everything is connected and the truth and fruits of a positive spirit of Love reveal their source, Love or Fear. The Chinese model of energy circuits reflect the process of discernment of Love.

I think all these power the body biochemistry of our blood and blood is sacred as it contains the forces of life for Love. Of course we know blood as a red liquid within our body but it is a sea of active cells working constantly to balance and harmonize the body for health and wellbeing as much as possible. If we have healthy thoughts and healthy lifestyle we assist the body to be able to live in the higher and more comfortable states of being that are Positive Love.

Let me expand these 7 Pillars of Positive Love for all. These 7 spirits of God, 7 requirements for making Love whole and complete have been discerned from the Book of Revelation Chapters 2 and 3 in accord with my other research. I have a whole thesis on these but I will summarize to keep it simple.

Love from Love comes the emotional and psychological states of kindness, mildness, goodness, patience, self control (not to sin) for inner peace with a quiet conscience for peace within the self as well as with others for joy, happiness, positive belief systems for faith, passion, will, desire for Love made whole with the ability for repentance and forgiveness for healing when a wrong has been done.

Faith from faith comes the emotional state of trust, knowing and assurance that Love will be a positive experience: 'Positive Love' will be and that people will be righteous and good and turn away from selfish sinful inclinations, therefore life will become positive, fulfilling and good. This gives positive goals with security, trust and assured hope of Love made whole in the future; this is faith.

Discernment from discernment comes choice, sorting, placing, differentiation, good or bad, right or wrong, halal or haram, healthy or toxin, positive or negative. Positive Love or negative fear. Knowing and understanding the differences for empowerment and self direction in accord with Love made positive and whole which is worthy of honour and praise.

Righteousness the right order, from righteousness comes clarity of direction, priority and fulfillment. An assurance of certainty of knowing which is the right way to act.

Consciousness From Love, faith, discernment and righteousness comes awareness which is consciousness. The ability to balance, to stabilize our bodies emotionally and physically and psychologically by following what is right for us in the whole context of Positive Love and fulfillment.
This allows us to have positive interactions with others to not be fearful by being in Positive Love and to remove stress which allows us to have positive relationships with others resulting with

Brotherly Love and Friendship, allows for positive relationships to blossom for peace and Love to prevail for

Peace, peaceful relationships with the self via a quiet conscience and with others via trust and faith, a tolerance and acceptance of others allowing us to receive communion of Love, a state of Positive Love which is not threatening, hurtful or painful in any way.

There is no need for fear of bad intent from another if all strive towards righteousness with faith for 'Positive Love' there by creating peace and unity among men for joy, happiness, patience, tolerance, security, safety, peace for paradise and Heaven on Earth, the state of bliss in Love, the ultimate state of being a spiritual being doing God's will in our human form attaining to rapture, Heaven on Earth with sin conquered, the stress and fear held in place trust and faith by virtue for whole Love to prevail for the promised land of fulfillment in us.

The magic in this is it is self creating. If we embody these refined positive states of being then they in turn create themselves because they only create a positive experience of life. 'The Creator of Love Causes Himself to Become' in us and is worthy of honor and praise and publication.

By living these very states of consciousness or being they create more of themselves. They are self creating at a quantum level, like attracting like, like creating like. Love that is Positive and whole manifested in us for conscious understanding.

Communion with Love communion with the whole spirit of Love for Love to prevail as a positive experience and the name of the whole spirit of Love is Jesus Christ, The Anointed One. There is only oneness in Love made whole and there can only be One God of Love which is truth for Love to set us all free from sin by submission to the commandments to Love God who is Love by observing his commandments. There is only One God is the first commandment and also the meaning of the Arabic name of God Allah and a Muslim is a person who submits their will to God for peace in accord with the Love and mercy of God. Islam means peace and I think if more people understood the Islamic teachings are in accord with the scriptures there would be much less Islamaphobia which in itself is a contradiction. If Islam means peace and a phobia is a fear then Islamaphobia means fear of peace and fear cannot reside with peace just as fear cannot reside with Love and peace only comes from Love. The 99 names or attributes of God in Islam are the same qualities of the God in scripture who's name means 'He who causes Love to become' ' whole in Love' for peace and all fruits of the spirit. Remember Jesus' words 'by their fruits we will know them' and if we find fruits of the spirit of Love and peace then we know their origin is with The One God of Love. Perhaps we would be better to seek the fruits consciously and not compete and it is a sin to purport divisions publicly as there is no division with God's Love. We are all beings made in the same manner and only with Love enthused from the whole spirit of Love do we then become Human beings able to live by spirit.

Sin falls short of Love by creating stress and fear responses taking us away from Love. This is a physiological autonomic nervous system response and is how our bodies are made, it is how we function and beyond our own control except by submission to Positive Love made whole in us in accord with God's Love for trust and peace to prevail.

The Chinese model of energy for the acupuncture energy system is reflective of theocratic order as is the structure of a horse herd. Indian models of creating peace and energy, the life force in the body reflect theocratic order. If we find Peace and Love and Friendship and Unity with Communion with Positive Love and Communion with Love in Peace and Joy we know the Love is there. We must remember God is Love and The Spirit of Love made whole for us to manifest His Love in us. We must seek the fruits and see the fruits without judgment and criticism, but also know that only consciousness of the origin of Love makes Love sustainable.

The way our bodies respond due to physiological and biological responses means that we 'all can be changed in the twinkling of an eye' 1st Corinthians 15:51-2 because the change from Love to fear or fear to Love is visible in the autonomic nerve wreath at the centre of the eye – as clearly visible in the iris (via iridology). The change is also clearly visible in thought patterns positive or negative. The state of being is clearly visible by the blood as either adrenaline and cortisol or endorphin blood. The blood is clearly visible by behaviours and hormonal traits, peace or conflict, flesh or spirit, Love or hate, patience and tolerance with Love or not.

We must not be fearful of 'the ologies' and the hands-on therapies because they work with the whole body to calm and sooth away stresses caused from hurts and pains. Some of these will have been caused by sin and as with the acts of the apostles contact with touch is needed to release the nervous system stress response for healing to occur. We must remember touch is meant to be a positive experience and not only associated with sexual experiences. Touch is meant to be a positive and natural experience and is very soothing and calming to all.

One thing worthy of note that always when a healing occurred with Jesus he said 'your faith has made you well'.

Remember faith is the assured expectation of good things and as a positive belief system for good healing can occur. Remember our thoughts are creative and what we think we create more of so ultimately only positive thought forms are worthy if we want trust and peace for security for joy and happiness and fulfillment of Love. Our thoughts are our choices and we have free will but the irony is without God's Love we can never attain to true peace and happiness with self or others. God's Love really is made perfect in us and this is our duty for Him and for others and self if we want to attain to Love which is what I think we are all seeking ultimately.

We must not be fearful of each other and our different names and ways but seek the whole spirit in each other and learning from each other is a great joy and education and one of the joys of travel. When we visit different cultures we see things done in different ways yet producing the same spirit of Love in completeness. Do not judge each other but see the unity of spirit of Love and share the joy. We are all One through Love.

To be or not be Love

It is funny how I thought it would be easy
I thought it would be easy;
I really thought it would be easy

I thought *you* would be delighted with the data analysis
the observations observed and the conclusions concluded are
conclusive,

They were quite simple really; the principles were not new,
they are not new, but I knew,
I could see that the science backed up the principles: –

It is fantastically obvious and obviously fantastic –
how could it not be? How could it not be? How can it not be?
It could not, not be, it had to be, it has to be, it will be...

I will tell you a little secret; it has to be,
it is the promise for life you see; What? You may well ask;

'To be or not to be' is the question - but it is so much more than a
question, to be is the answer to everything:

When we are not being true, we are being something else,
something we are not meant to be,
something we are not, therefore a lie;

A lie is not our truth and is not Love, Not Love, Not Love.

Not Love is not being Love. Not Love is not being. Not Love is not
being Love; which is not Love.

You see it is Love we are meant to be and Love needs no rules to be,
except Love...

Love rules Love and causes Love to become;

Love is never hurtful or unkind. Love needs to be and Love has to
be, it is the only way to be,

But hey - it is not easy in a world full of vices wanting to
entices us away from Love, away from Love, away from Love.

How can it be that you and me fall short, are short changed
the dream?
The dream of Love becoming One; Love becoming whole
Love?

Well only by not being Love and allowing not Love to be
which is not heavenly and it is not being Love in being;

It is not being Love; it is not being Love which is not being;

This is how we be, by being Love, by being Love enthused to make
us optimistic positive beings with hope of Love,

Faith in Love, certainty in Love, for Love to be enthused beings,
human beings, loving beings, happy beings

and so it goes on ad infinitum, to infinity and beyond:
Eternal; So be Love;

Love in being: To be is the only answer to Love
to infuse Love to enthuse Love for Love to be enthused,
infused into us to be Love.

So Be It. Amen, Ameen. Shalom, Namaste, Peace to all.

Some of the workings out of the Sacred Secret Seven Spirits of God

The Seven Spirits of God as discerned from Revelation 2 and 3.
Seven Colours of the rainbow - rainbow covenant, seven notes of the musical scale
Proverbs 9:1 says 'True wisdom has built its house, it has hewn out its seven pillars'.
Revelation 1:20 As for the sacred secret of the seven stars that you saw upon my right hand, and [of] the seven golden lamp stands: The seven stars mean [the] angels of the seven congregations, and the seven lamp stands mean seven congregations.
The seven congregations: Ephesus, Smyrna, Pergamum, Thyatira, Sardis, Philadelphia, Laodicea
The seven spirits are the keys to conquer death of the spirit and Hades.
Revelation 1:17….."Do not be fearful. I am the First and the Last, 18 and the living one; and I became dead, but, look! I am living forever and ever, and I have the keys of death and Ha'des.
Revelation 1:1 A revelation by Jesus Christ, which God gave him, to show his slaves the things that must shortly take place.
New Heavens and New Earth
'Thy will be done on earth as it is in heaven' the Heavenly organisation of spirit creatures, the heavenly organisation of emotions and psychological though patterns.

	1 **To Ephesus**
Congregation	
Golden Lamp stands	
7 Stars	Granted to eat of the Tree of Life in
the paradise of God	
Messengers	
Angels	'Paradise: Heaven; region or state of supreme bliss; garden of Eden' pocket Oxford dictionary. The Anandamide bliss molecule attained only though naturally occurring endorphin blood through obedience to God's Love made whole in us by turning away from sin.
Commendations	The Ephesians were righteous
Good Attributes	loving good, testing false apostles,
finding liars	
	enduring, not growing weary hating sects and divisions.
Constructive Criticism	
	They had lost the love they had at
first	
	They needed to love God with Whole heart, whole soul, whole mind and whole strength to Love others to walk in Love Remember from what you have fallen and repent, do your former good deeds
Spirit	To repent, be sorry, turn around, regain the fruits and spirit of Love
Positive Emotions	To cultivate enthusiasm, love, passionate, with feeling, compassion, and understanding

Negative Emotions   Cold, unfeeling, without heart,
judgmental
to overcome   empathy and compassion
forgotten.

1st Spirit of Love and Light : Love

Love: feeling, sense, compassion, enthusiasm, keep trying,
repent and try again, seek, persist a positive outcome. Love is
always a Positive state of being with no fear except of
disobedience to Love which is the ultimate goal for and of
human fulfilment of experience thereby God.
Colour: Red Ray
Musical Note: C
Sense: Smell
Root Chakra, energy centre of the body
Metal: Lead, heaviness, grounded, rooted, secure, stable
Endocrine Glands: for sexuality, reproduction and pituitary.
Foundation Stone: Jasper, courage for seeking Love which
enhances the senses which increases learning, gives protection
by knowledge, discernment sorting, understanding,
satisfaction, warmth, comfort and contentment in a positive
order.

Congregation	**2 To Smyrna**
Golden Lamp Stands	
7 Stars	Crown of Life
Messengers	
Angels	
Goals/Aim	
Commendations	Endured persecution
Good Attributes	Proved faithful
Constructive Criticism	Materially poor but spiritually rich
Spirit	Faith, hope
Positive emotion	Trust
Negative emotion	Fear

2nd Spirit of Love and Light : Faith

Faith includes hope, trust and endurance for Love which is always a Positive state of being with no fear except of disobedience to Love which is the ultimate goal for and of human fulfilment of experience thereby God. Hebrews 11:1 says 'Faith is the assured expectation of the things hope for, the evident demonstration of things not yet beheld'. A positive belief system in the fulfilment of Love, God's Love made whole in us and others for a positive state of Love to prevail in all for Heaven and Peace on Earth.

Colour: Orange Ray

Musical Note: D

Sense: Taste

Sacral Chakra, energy centre of the body, creative, reproductive.

Metal: Tin.

Endocrine Gland: Ovaries and Testes for sexuality, reproduction and Pituitary.

Foundation Stone: Sapphire; loyalty love, direction, clarity and communication, hope, strength, purpose, direction, focus, commitment to a positive out come which is Love.

Golden Lamp Stands

7 Stars	Hidden Manna
Messengers	White pebble with new name on it
Angels	Manna food provisions from God
Goals/Aim	food, nourishment, banquet

Commendations
Good attributes

Constructive Criticism	Sectarianism false worship, Emperor worship Divided
Spirit	Divisive, fallible
Positive Emotion	Faith, Self Control and Focus
Negative Emotion goal	Divisive, no unity, no common

3rd Spirit of Love and Light: Discernment

Discernment through accurate knowledge of the positive state of thinking and being in Love and Faith. Discernment, sorts, accepts the good rejects the bad realises only one God who cause Oneness though causing Love to become whole in spirit in us: united, totality, clear message and understanding. Acceptance and rejection, food, nutrient for sustaining health and well being or toxin for elimination by detoxification. Physical and spiritual foods including a positive belief system in the fulfilment of Love, God's Love made whole in us and others for a positive state of Love to prevail in all for Heaven and Peace on Earth.

Colour: Yellow Ray

Musical Note: E

Sense: Sight

Chakra: Solar Plexus energy centre of the body, creative, reproductive.

Metal: Iron, energy, power, empowerment.

Endocrine Gland: Pituitary, Spleen, Pancreas and Kidneys.

Foundation Stone: Chalcedony; soothes irritations emotional and physical, spirit overcomes fleshly reactions, brings balance, happiness, joy, discernment, suppleness, flexibility, strength and commitment to a positive outcome which is Love which enhances senses which increases learning, gives protection by knowledge, discernment, sorting, understanding, satisfaction, warmth, comfort and contentment in a righteous order for the whole state of Love to prevail.

Congregation	4 **To Thyatira**
Golden Lamp Stands	
7 Stars	Authority over nations
Messengers	Shepherd with iron rod
Angels	break like clay pieces
Goals/Aim	fragile, brittle.
Commendations	Good deeds, love and faith,
ministry	
Good Attributes	and endurance
Wrong values	Idolatry, fornication, tolerance of
	Jezebel, selling, sold out
Constructive Criticism	
Spirit	Judged by heart and kidneys
	Love, the motive and discernment,
	Love with faith for Love to be
	made whole for more Love or fear
	and doubt, negativity, faithless,
	hopeless, fleshly, toxicity versus
	potential of purity of spirit of love
	made whole by righteousness.
Positive Emotion	Knowing what is right and wrong,
discernment,	
	choice, choosing right, righteous
Negative Emotion	Confusion, ignorance, senseless

4th Spirit of Love and Light: Righteousness

Righteousness; organised, order, theocratic order, right order, right motives and right choices, halal, righteous.
Colour: Green Ray
Musical Note: F
Sense: Feeling, Touch
Chakra: Heart energy centre of the body, creative, reproductive.
Metal: Copper, vascular strength .
Endocrine Gland: Pituitary, heart, thymus,adrenal.
Foundation Stone: Emerald for peace, wisdom, understanding, emotions balanced, stable, compassionate, kind and loving for a positive belief system in the fulfilment of Love, God's Love made whole in us and others for a positive state of Love to prevail in all for Heaven and Peace on Earth. Love enhances senses which increases learning, gives protection by knowledge, discernment sorting, understanding, satisfaction, warmth, comfort and contentment in a righteous order for the whole and positive state of Love to prevail.

| Congregation | 5 **To Sardis** |
| Golden Lamp Stands | |

7 Stars	Untainted righteousness
Messengers	Spirit, energy, tent of God with
mankind	
Angels	outer garments made white
Goals/Aim	Book of Life
Commendations	Remember
Good attributes	

Constructive Criticism	To become watchful, wake up,
	keep their senses, remember how
	you learnt.
Spirit	Forgetfulness, desensitised,
insensitive, missing the point	

| Positive Emotion | Protection, safety, security, trust |

Negative Emotion	Hypocritical, double standards,
	spiritually dead, physically
	insensitive.

5th Spirit of Love and Light: Consciousness

Consciousness, righteousness, consciousness,   knowing what is right and acting in accordance with what is right even if we get it wrong, there is a right way to act – to repent and try again, to re think and strive for the spirit of Love that is whole.

Colour: Blue Ray

Musical Note: G

Sense: Auditory, ears and voice

Foundation Stone: Sardonyx and Sardius, wrestlings with good and bad, haram and halal for for consciousness and forgiveness for expression and trust for others to be kind and loving for a positive belief system in the fulfilment of Love, God's Love made whole in us and others for a positive state of Love to prevail in all for Heaven and Peace on Earth.

Chakra: Throat energy centre of the body, expression, voice.

Metal: Mercury, vascular strength .

Endocrine Gland: Pituitary, thyroid, para-thyroids.

Consciousness gives information for reasoning via enhanced senses which increase righteous learning and give protection by knowledge, discernment sorting, understanding, satisfaction, warmth, comfort and contentment in a righteous order for the whole and positive state of Love to prevail for communicating and sharing.

Congregation
Golden lamp stands

7 Stars   Brotherly affection
Messengers   Keys of David
Angels   Will be kept from the hour
of test
Goals/Aim
Commendations   Keep on holding to what
you have
Good Attributes   So no one can take your
crown
                                      Crown of Life is via Love

and Faith
Constructive Criticism   Endurance
Spirit   Protected

Positive Emotion   Love faith endurance, seen
the right   way
and taking the opportunity to act
                                      Righteously.

Negative Emotion

6th Spirit of Love and Light: Peaceful Brotherly Love and Friendship

Recognition of theocratic order, enduring and active in Love and Faith there by conforming to the right order by positive choices with respect to the One God who causes Love to become made whole in us by Love of God, others and self, theocratic order resulting in a harmonious spirit of unity for integrity and peace with self, others and God.

Colour: Indigo Ray

Musical Note: A

Sense: Clarity, Vision, Light, Enlightenment, Understanding, Imagination, Intuition, Consciousness.

Chakra: Third Eye, Pineal, Pituitary.

Metal: Silver, antisceptic .

Endocrine Gland: Pituitary, Pineal, Melatonin.

Foundation Stone: Hyacynth, Sapphire for trust and faith for kindness and Love for a positive belief system in the fulfilment of Love, God's Love made whole in us and others for a positive state of Love to prevail in all for Heaven and Peace on Earth. Blue for communication and openness, honesty, truth, integrity, knowing right from wrong and acting accordingly with righteousness for loyalty for peace and friendship and peaceful relations with fellow men. An altruistic positive state of Love enhances senses which increases learning, gives protection by knowledge, discernment sorting, understanding, satisfaction, warmth, comfort and contentment in a righteous order for the whole and positive state of Love to prevail.

Congregation	7 **To Laodicea**
Golden Lamp Stands	
7 Stars	Lukewarm, neither hot nor cold
Messengers	Indifferent
Angels	Materially rich & comfortable
Goals/Aim	
Commendations	The one that conquers I will grant to sit down with me on my throne, even
Good attributes my	as I conquered and sat down with
	Father on His throne.
Constructive Criticism	Buy from me gold refined by fire, buy white outer garments to become dressed, buy eye salve to help you see
Spirit	communication Jesus standing knocking at door, let him in and take the evening meal together, communion,
Positive Emotion	Acceptance, recognition
Negative Emotion	Closed, blind, ignorant, unconscious, do not know they are miserable, pitiable and poor and blind and naked.

7th Spirit of Love and Light: Unity, Communion with The Oneness of Love

Acceptance of the Lord Jesus there by acceptance of The One God of Love who causes Love to become whole in us: Gods will being done 'on earth as it is in heaven', unity, communion by accurate knowledge, discernment, empowered with righteous choices, clarity of vision for positive life with Love made whole through anointing with The Whole Spirit namely Jesus Christ, Love of fellow men and women and children, man made kind and all God's good creation with Love and respect to self all with a positive outcome for life, for cultivating a spirit for all the fruits namely Love, Joy, Patience, Kindness, Goodness, Faith, Mildness, Self Control 9 not to sin) which leads to a quiet conscience with the self which gives Peace, Joy and Happiness which stabilises positive body biochemistry for health, happiness and rejoicing with the truth, for a whole spirit of Love; The Holy Spirit; a gift from God for life of the spirit to be maintained, everlasting, Amen,
Colour: Violet Ray
Musical Note: B
Sense: Clarity, Enlightenment, Understanding, Imagination Consciousness, Contemplation.
Chakra: Crown, Pituitary, pineal and whole endocrine system.
Metal: Gold, Positive flow.
Endocrine Gland: Pituitary, Pineal, Melatonin.

Foundation Stone: Amethyst, Diamond; truth, calm, knowledgeable, refined, purified, regenerated, organized and content, firm, secure, happy, whole, sound for trust and faith for kindness and Love for a positive belief system in the fulfillment of Love, God's Love made whole in us and others for a positive state of Love to prevail in all for Heaven and Peace on Earth. Blue for communication and openness, honesty, truth, integrity, knowing right from wrong and acting accordingly with righteousness for loyalty for peace and friendship and peaceful relations with fellow men. An altruistic positive state of Love enhances senses which increases learning, gives protection by knowledge, discernment sorting, understanding, satisfaction, warmth, comfort and contentment in a righteous order for the whole and positive state of Love to prevail within the self and with out with others for Peace with self and peace with others for Peace with God via a quiet conscience for 'the peace of God that excels all thought' Philippians 4:7.

Conclusion of the Seven Spirits of Love and Light: The Seven Spirits of God.

1st Spirit of Love and Light: Love, feeling, sense, compassion, enthusiasm, repentance, forgiveness, try again.

2nd Spirit of Love and Light: Faith, hope, trust and endurance, creative

3rd Spirit of Love and Light: discernment by accurate knowledge of Love and Faith gives discernment, sorts, accepts the good rejects the bad, only one God, unity.

4th Spirit of Love and Light: Righteousness organised, order, theocratic order, right order, right motives and right choices, righteous.
5th Spirit of Love and Light: Consciousness, righteousness, consciousness,   knowing what is right and acting in accordance with what is right even if we get it wrong, there is a right way to act – to repent and try again, re think, spirit that is whole   forgiveness
6th Spirit of Love and Light: Consciousness;   recognition of theocratic order, enduring and active in love and faith there by conforming to the right order by positive choices with respect to Jehovah God, others and self, theocratic order resulting in a harmonious spirit of unity for integrity and peace

7th Spirit of Love and Light: Unity by communion with The Oneness of Love acceptance of the whole spirit namely Jesus Christ there by acceptance of the God of Love who causes Love to become whole in us; God's will being 'done on Earth as it is in Heaven', unity, communion with accurate knowledge, discernment, empowered with righteous choices, clarity of vision for positive life for Love of God through Jesus Christ, Love of fellow men and women, mankind and all God's good creation with Love and respect to self all with a positive outcome for life, for cultivated spirit, for Love, Joy, Patience, Kindness, Goodness, Faith, Mildness, Self Control (to turn away from sin) which leads to a quiet conscience which gives peace, joy and happiness which stabilizes positive body biochemistry for health, happiness and rejoicing with the truth, for The Holy Spirit; the gift from God for life of the spirit to be everlasting;   Amen.

7 SPIRITS OF GOD

LOVE	will, desire, repentance
FAITH	knowing, trust, assurance
DISCERNMENT	choice, sorting, placing
RIGHT ORDER	righteous, sorted
CONSCIOUSNESS	awareness, knowing
BROTHERLY LOVE	giving, sharing
ACCEPTANCE	receiving, communion

For unity, joy, happiness and peace for life.

Death of the spirit of Love is guilt, shame, lies, denial, activated by the conscience.

The only release is by repentance and turning away from stressful ways, having repentance for forgiveness and the only way back to Love as a positive state of being in us hence God is Love, Love is the ultimate state of being for us.

These positive aspects of emotional and spiritual states of being and consciousness do correspond with the energy centre's of the body known as chakras which are influential in glandular and hormone function. In healing the energy is affected before the physical so an ailment will have occurred in the aura before manifesting physically. Likewise repairing the energy flow and aura will in time repair the body. This is how crystals, magnets and essences can influence the state of being of the body, working at homeopathic levels of resonance in the energy flows of the body.

Galatians 5:22 Fruits of the Spirit for Peace, happiness, bliss
Heaven on Earth – Rapture   Oneness, Completeness
Love, Joy, Faith, Kindness, Mildness, Goodness,
Patience, self Control (not to sin) Peace
God - who is Love
Whole spirit anointed
Love made Whole
Positive Love
Eternal Life of the spirit
Oneness Life
Communion with One Love
Brotherly Love, Unity
Consciousness, understanding,
Love, Faith, discernment
Right Way, Narrow Road, Halal

Love   Faith   Discernment
God laws   our belief systems   leading to:

Not right way, Broad way, Haram
Indulgence of sinful, abusive behaviours
Lawlessness , permission of evil, chaos
Gnashing of teeth, destructive,
Unconscious, dead, no understanding
No brotherly love, frictions,
Conflict, strife angers,
Jealousy
Negative, cut off, selfish fear,
Stress sin War
No Love, No Peace
Divided, split
Conflict
Fleshly Traits Galatians 5:19

****

Seven Chakras, Colour and the Body

Here we enter into energy, subtle bodies and vibration; light, colour and auras. These are the vibes we can feel even though may not be able to visually see, yet! They are the elephant in the room. Some people especially healers and artists can see auras and chakra colours around the body and living organisms and modern imaging techniques are proving their existence. In my experience I see them sometimes, but not all the time. As a child I was very aware of them. I think children can see them but tune out of that ability with physical distractions like television, yet it is the sense of defocus, a form of meditation by mind clearing that reveals the colours. We can feel energy with our senses if we listen and tune into them and now science has instruments able to measure them. (When I first wrote this book there was not the availability of measures of these, but in the last twenty plus years there has been huge progress in the medical and scientific worlds. Think of ultra sound scans and MRI scans).

We know magnetic, electromagnetic gravity electricity nucleic and sub nuclear force fields exist and I am sure there are many more. It is here we enter into quantum physics and the energy fields of vibration. This quantum world is becoming more known about through many media channels and for me is where emotion guides our sense of being. Personally I do not agree with Stephen Hawkins that time has a beginning or end, I think time is a very human measurement and I think the universe is ever changing, I think it expands and contracts in the same way we breath and the same way the tide ebbs and flows and is just the way the elements interact with each other creating light and dark, light and density and new light and energy.

Deepak Chopra defines 'A quantum defined as the basic unit of matter or energy, is from 10,000,000 to 100,000,000 times smaller than the smallest atom. At this level where matter and energy are interchangeable true healing begins.'

Healing is available to all as it operates from a deep level of spiritual love, faith and hope acted upon. We all have this ability as it is ultimately a vibration of positive thought forms which by themselves are creative. I think ultimately that healing is a process of facing uncomfortable truths which are contrary to the state of alignment and of love with in us, within our cells and energy flows of the body.

Living organisms are surrounded by bio-electrical fields which are constantly changing with life. The emotions reveal stresses and the thought patterns determine the emotions and create a profile of what is going on for the person or animal, or any life form. Think of this as the vibe or atmosphere, a good atmosphere or vibe or a bad one, a positive one or a negative one, This is the elephant in the room because energy does not lie. The electrical field of the body joins us with the outside world and creates a new world which depends on the nature of the relationships, positive or negative. Electrical fields become one so when we are with others our energy fields combine and create a new energy fields. These are what create herds in animals and form organisations through united thought and behaviours.

We must also remember to include the obvious forces of light, dark and sound as they influence our body, mind and spirit profoundly.

So, we all have a physical body that we can see, feel and touch. On from the physical body there are electromagnetic energy lines known as meridians which form the structure of traditional Chinese medicine. The meridians are closely linked to our nerve pathways. Think of the nerve pathway as a series of electrical messages passing through the body most probably at the speed of light and beyond. All electrical wires, physical or biological and even atomic will have an energy field surrounding it, this is the electromagnetic field. From this electromagnetic field the energy arises movement and swirls that become what are known as chakras. These are points of energy intake that have positive and negative polarity and they swirl like a wheel in motion. The name chakra originates from a Sanskrit word meaning wheel and the patterns resemble flowers in particular the lotus blossom with several petals. Also there are many interpretations in art and healing patterns and I think this is also how gemstones can make such profound changes in healing. It is the genetic patterns of the elements that make up minerals and gemstones that affect and effect all life forms. I think it is at this level of understanding that many of the world's religions share common ground and it is these similarities that should be focused and united on. Stress and trauma will affect the flow of these energies and reduce the vibration of love and light thereby creating a loss of vitality and ultimately creating darkness. Stress and trauma change the flow of energy and in some cases reverse the flow of love. Think of a sun versus a black hole, a sun being light and warm and emitting energy and a black hole being dark, dense and heavy sapping light and energy. It is the very creative process of life and the destructive process of atrophy which are a part of all life. In theory if we can create positive life experiences based on love and happiness then our energy will be strong and positive and light which then creates healthier, happier cells which function optimally for health and well being. This in turn keeps the body from degenerative conditions. This means we retain or reclaim with healing our youthful glow.

Where there is stress then there is disruption to the positive flow which creates blocks and imbalances in our cells and body systems. These are what need to be turned around for healing to occur and for positive flows of energy to be re-established. There are many incidences of healing occurring through people changing a negative life course and choosing a new and positive one. It can be that simple. There are also many incidences of people's lives being turned around through counselling, healthier life styles and self awareness and improvement with self care and nourishing treatments with faith. Chakras are swirls of energy with different vibrations producing different colours. When we are resonating with love there is lots of colour which is light. When there is an absence of love or colour then there is a lack of light therefore more dark and density which is heavy and negative. Here I give a brief and concise summary of the chakras of the body. When we think in quantum terms of light they are not mystical or complicated at all.

The Chakras

First of all what is colour? Black is sometimes known as the absence of colour and colour is what makes up the light spectrum. However Black can be made up of all the colours and white can be the absence of colour too. The answer can depend on what type of colour is being looked at. The energy of colour in the light spectrum is different to the makeup of colour in the physical world as in the makeup of paints which derives its colours from elements and minerals. Here I am looking at colour in the light spectrum. It may be that the difference in colour in the different spectrums is an excellent analogy of how light affects our physical functions and body. The chakra system is an ancient Indian concept used to explain energy currents in the body and is common practice in yoga and many forms of meditation. The chakras form a rainbow of colour through the body and indeed when these are all swirling together we do find the positive state of love which becomes golden. Indeed the pot of gold at the end of the rainbow and the heavenly city of God/love which is paved with gold. Can this really be? How can it be? You may well ask! I think the chakras emanate from and influence the glands which they are situated next to. Just as the meridians reflect the nervous system, the chakras reflect the glandular system and vice versa. It is the glandular system which determine our hormones and our blood chemistry thereby our health and well being, or not.

When all our chakras are in balance we are in a state of Positive Love and happiness that we can share. We are energised and full of positivity, creativity and full of life, health and well being. We are resonating with colour and light and oneness with self and the universe. We are one by having no separation or division with self. We are one. We are whole. Whole in the spirit of love. Holy. Full of loves spirit. Oneness. No divisions within or without. One having learnt loyalty to self and love, God, repentance and forgiveness as in Joseph and his technicolour dream coat. Colour faith and positivity with love is life. All else falls short of love. Sadly few resonate with this true joy and here is the key to many ailments related to emotional disturbances within the body and mind. We do not need science to create drugs to mask our misalignments, we need to seek the Positive Love and fulfilment of God's love by learning from our wrongs and putting right. All this is emotional feelings we can gain control off with love and trust, hope and faith. Abuse and corruption makes this difficult and body systems have to be reset. Prevention is always better than cure, but with counsel of love made worthy then we can attain to peace through the whole love of Jesus Christ manifested in us, our behaviours and morals as in Isaiah 9.6.

Chakra Colours and Positions: The Crown Chakra

The crown chakra reflects the life force or soul and links with divine intelligence within and without.

Location: Top of head

Colour: Violet, Purple

Gemstone: Amethyst, Diamond

Planet: Uranus

Element: Gold

Sense: Thought

Organ: Brain

Gland: Pituitary and Pineal which control the glandular secretions, central nervous system, stress response and movement of the cerebral spinal fluid, spine, skin and hair.

Spiritual and emotional states: Calmness, confidence, balance, wisdom, letting go, release, and peace leading to self awareness, self consciousness. It homes the will and the will to do good and connect with self, others and higher being, God, Love, self consciousness of mind, body and spirit.

 Negative traits: loss of will, loss of faith, loss of hope, depression, mental disorders, seizures, shaking, nervous disorders, anxieties.

The Brow Chakra

Location: Forehead
Colour: Indigo
Gemstones: Amethyst, pearl, blue fluorite, white fluorite.
Planet: Jupiter
Element: Silver
Sense: Intuition
Organ: Brain
Gland: Pituitary & Pineal
Spiritual and emotional states: Sleeping, walking, daylight, higher mental self, clarity, vision, intuition seeing the light. Also known as the third eye and the pineal gland responds to light and the light of understanding through reason. Possibly the symbol of the mythical unicorn with a spiral energy moving forward for good.
Negative traits: confusion, dark, headaches, eyesight problems, vision, hormonal.

The Throat Chakra

Location: Throat and neck
Colour: Blue
Gemstones: Turquoise, Sapphire, Aquamarine, Lapis Lazuli
Planet: Mercury
Element: Heavens, ether
Sense: Speech, taste
Organ: Tongue, lung, intestines
Gland: Salivary Thyroid
Spiritual and emotional states: Communication, expression, release, creativity, acceptance, healing, change, freedom, free speech, voice.
Ability to metabolise physically, mentally and emotionally, reason.
Negative traits: inhibition, unable to express self, isolation, disconnected, digestive problems, frustrations, not finding voice, asthma, chest problems, throat problems, eating disorders, digestive problems.

The Heart Chakra

Location: Chest
Colour: Green
Gemstones: Emerald, Azurite, Jade Tourmaline
Planet: Venus
Element: Air
Sense: Touch, feeling
Organ: Heart
Gland: Heart, Thymus
Spiritual and emotional states: of love, The Golden Rule, love others as self, as God or the greater good, self love and shared love, environment care, feelings, sharing, uniting, forgiveness, tenderness, balance, energy, vitality, joy, giving and receiving. Strengthens immune system, congruence.
Negative traits: hurt, bitterness, resentments, rejection, heart disease, immune disease, allergies, cancers.

The Solar Plexus Chakra

Location: Navel, Belly
Colour: Yellow
Gemstones: Topaz
Planet: Mars - Sun
Element: Fire
Sense: Sight
Organ: Kidney
Gland: Adrenal
Spiritual and emotional states: Empowerment, freedom from negative emotions, knowing, certainty, will power, focus, positive outlook, faith. vitality and energy, self worth truth, pain free.
Negative traits: anger, resentment, unworthiness, guilt, loss of self worth, loss of own power, deflated, sad, emotional problems, depression, stress and liver, spleen, pancreas and stomach problems.

The Sacral Chakra

Location: Sacral, hips.
Colour: Orange
Gemstones: Topaz, Jasper, Ruby
Planet: Moon
Element: Water
Sense: Awareness, self respect
Organ: Womb
Gland: Uterus, Ovaries
Spiritual and emotional states: security, nurturing, creativity, awareness, desire, procreation, children, family, self respect, balance, space, safety.
Negative traits: possessiveness, commitment problems, blurred boundaries, dependant, separation issues, clinging on, menstrual problems, bowel problems.

The Root Chakra

Location: Coccyx, base of spine and perineum.
Colour: Red
Gemstones: Jasper, Ruby, bloodstone, Onyx
Planet: Saturn
Element: Earth
Sense: Common sense, combined senses attraction, sexual desire.
Organ: Sex organs
Gland: Testes and ovaries
Spiritual and emotional states: grounded, stability, acceptance, self preservation, physical strength, balance, commonsense, connectedness, security, confidence, self awareness, natural sexual feelings.
Negative traits: stress, insecurity, inferiority, fear, destabilised, rejection, guilt, bowel disorders, sexual disorders.

From a healing perspective Chakras are one area where energy medicine therapists and healers work to restore the flow of energy between these spinning wheels of energy. With stress and illness the flow of the individual chakras becomes blocked. By placing our hands above the energy centres the energy will interact and start to move again. Consciously by adding in frequencies of colour and vibration the frequencies of resonance are raised. Crystals match these vibrations and frequencies because they are made up of the same elements.

Wonder, Amazement and the Imagination

Wonder, amazement and delight are all states of being that come from our right brain creative area and they transcend day to day life. Are they emotional states of being? Faith, trust, hope, belief patterns, right brain stimulation, dreams, goals, direction of will, the paradise hope, optimism, right.

Body Flesh Experience affects mind through nervous system and neuro chemicals through the blood. Discernment affects nervous system, messages, understandings, truths, reality. Understanding is relevant to knowledge, the benchmarks measured with accurate knowledge is the right benchmark to understand from, understanding from our creator. He knows how we work in mind and body in order to get to positive spirit.

What does it really mean to be human? I think to be human means to cultivate Godly qualities of loving kindness to others which in turn benefits and brings hope, trust and joy to others and also to the self which also benefits the greater good whom some call God and is based on creating love being positive and kind, Positive Love. This creates positive energy for well being for all and is how there really is more joy in giving. Being human is not displaying selfish survival instincts or behaviours for self survival as these are based in stress and fear with no trust or faith. the requirement is of course in an ideal world that trust and faith for Love and Peace are reciprocal behaviours.

When I was at school, if we had detention from a certain teacher, we had to write lines 'Manners Maketh Man' (a quote from William Horman 's Latin grammar text book Vulgaria written in 1519.)

****

It was not until I was an adult and out in the real world that I realised no manners equals rude which is inconsiderate of another being.

Manners are respectful and treating others how we would like to be treated by considering another person or being in our space. I really appreciate the lesson learned from those lines.

We choose how to be but we do need to educate compassion for the greater good of all because it needs trust and security to feel safe and not go into a fear based survival reaction. This is why it is so vital that our governments provide provisions for social security for all in the form of facilities, education and environment that cultivates good for all.

Evolution – I see mankind is evolving in conscious awareness. Waking up the brain, uniting the brain hemispheres to move away from primitive traits and refining himself as loving, kind, compassionate, just and fair beings living by and in spirit, not only flesh. This benefits all, everyone and everything. This is man in God's image. We are constantly evolving and learning. Could Darwin's evolution theory be interpreted as racist? Creation was before evolution and we are still evolving and creating.

Enthusiasm; The name human being originates from enthuse which means to be with God, literally translated it means God in being, God present, God in the now. Only if we consider Him, His values and laws can this be true. If God is Love and Light then does it not make sense that the positive emotional qualities of Love and Light are creating Love and Light in us. What we put in we get out.

****

Enthusiasm is us infused with love, hope, joy and faith in happiness and fulfilment. Positive qualities of Love in us from learning love for Love. Love worthy of honour in our being or God in our being because who would not want to cultivate this most wonderful state of being?

The following poem is designed to show the unity of energy as a creative force for the energy of Love and Light in us which because of it's positive emotional profile and vibrancy through colour making sound and whole is ultimately the force of Oneness in us and with everything, a force worthy of cultivating and focusing on, thereby a God.

A Philosophical Pythagoras Poem for Creating Healing Love and Light

Everything and nothing, an eve of no and thing, particles of nothingness
like black is every colour and at the same time an absence of colour
dark and dense, a vacuum, opposite to light
like light emits a source of no vacuum but a flow like a river of energy giving and making a river of Love
hydrogen and oxygen, helium from above, somewhere in the heavens that are there
light removed from the dark black, separated from the chaos creating order, creating two, opposition that lives in us too as positive and negative, lightness and dark, lightness and heaviness that needs
a spark of sparkling stars like sparklers sparkling on an autumn night
magnesium explosions like Coq10 in our hearts
that we can only see with an absence of day in the dark night
becoming the day through dawn
through mellow yellows and orange pinks, a rising fireball that makes me think
there must be something,   something that makes us see
something from this chemistry in this mystery of physics and geometry giving us a matrix for life, something in this chaotic soup of everything and no thing
heaviness and light and darkness and light and night and day and wrong and right and dim and bright light stars guiding to gold and myrrh and frankincense;

Frank in   sense: senses coming together like a village common for common good for the community to commune,
senses coming together making six and seven rays of input making whole, whole and holes like no and every thing
like string strung strong theories theorising everything
when some things are beyond theories, beyond measure like pleasing pleasures that are so beyond measure except by the feeling the feeling of being alive;

****

of cells tingling, vibrations communicating, connecting, making,
building creating light and light energy of gifting abundance and
dark and dark energy of density and
vacuums of giving or taking;
like mathematics,
adding up to profit or loss, multiplying what you give,
attracting more of every thing or no thing;

Health and wealth or ills and pills creating the windowsills we sit
and view our life from
the rectangular, arched or round window,
a glass half full or empty
packed full of crystals and grains of sand and just when you think it
can contain no more,   it can be filled with water
and add some heat and you can make clouds
 and add some light and you can make a rainbow that you can see;

Who says we can't see the light?

Because light has colour, rays ordered and separated into
frequencies of vibration
resonance, colours making sound that we can hear,
filling voids with healing light
frequencies making sound, making whole, harmonising Love.

Love capturing crystal rainbows for healing life
rain bowing,   light arching light to earth
creating visions of hope, colours that we can see
with an absence of dark,
with an absence of no and everything.

Chapter 10

Israel or Is Real

The way to fulfillment of the human being, fulfillment of the spirit of Love, making Love whole in spirit, anointed with the whole spirit of Love for the fruits of the spirit to abound for Love.

From the 7 Spirits for Positive Love discerned from Revelation we can understand the relevance of Israel and New Jerusalem in a new way. The names of the sons of Israel all have meaning that when linked together reveal the consciousness for attaining to the whole spirit of Love.

Judah means a son lauded.

Reuben means to see the son who is love.

Gad means good fortune, positive love and blessings.

Asher means happiness, love and faith, a positive form of love.

Naphtali means my wrestling's - the fight against fearful, faithless sinful inclinations of the flesh which take away from the positive states of love and happiness and faith thus creating stress and fear and conflict in the self and others. The choices we make every moment of every day to act morally and righteously for the positive good of everyone, or to act selfishly for self gain. When we act morally for good we do still attain to personnel fulfillment. Everyone has fulfillment with trust and security knowing the intention is good and positive. Wrestlings of good or evil, positive and negative, all or self, halal or haram, God or satan, flesh or spirit, sin or God's Love etc.

****

Manasseh means to make forgetful, to forgive.

Simeon means a listener; he hears and reasons for understanding and compassion for another.

Levi means adherence and sticks to, committed and loyal.

Issachar is the rewarder with peace and communion of spirit.

Zebulun means tolerance and goodwill, patience and understanding for peace.

Joseph means may Jah add, may Love be increased to understand the positive force of the spirit of Love for creating Love and honoring its states of being by turning away from sin. Joseph is a fine example of repelling sin and transcending sinful behaviours from others. Joseph shows us how to create Positive Love in us for us, for each other for everyone, others and self. A perfect measure, all for one and one for all which does increase Love, which increases Jah in all our lives.

Benjamin means son of my mourning. If we mourn our grief and pain we can heal our spirit which can energize our bodies for love and life. If we ignore or suppress our grief and pain we suffer and the grief and pain will manifest in physical ways. We need to consciously process our emotional wounds, our psychological fears and painful aches and injuries of the flesh for a restoration of Positive Love in us, for healing of our mind, body and spirit. We can do this consciously with reason, forgiveness and understanding. It is within our power to help ourselves. Practicing Positive Love brings peace and happiness, peace and goodwill for us all resulting in Ephraim who's name means doubly fruitful for two fold peace which is the meaning of the name Jerusalem.

****

Revelation tribes order 144,000 Spiritual Jerusalem
Tribes, meanings and matched with the fruits of the spirit
Galatians 5:22.

Judah : lauded   JHVH: **He who causes to become**

Reuben: See a son   Jesus Christ: **Anointed**

Gad: Good Fortune   Love Positive blessings
                                        Whole spirit of-Love
Asher: Happiness   Love Positive **Joy**
                                                Happy-**Faith**
Naphtali: My wrestling's: fight against sinful   inclinations
                                                Self Control
Manasseh: Making Forgetful   Forgiveness   Hope, Faith
                                                Patience
Simeon: hearing   Active Listening,
                        Understanding, Compassion
Levi: Adhering   Committing, Baptising   **Kindness**
Issachar: Rewarder   Love, Peace, **Goodness**

Zebulun: Tolerance   Goodwill   **Mildness**

Joseph : Jah Increased, Love increased, **Peace** increased
                        Understanding God's will for us.

Benjamin: Son of my mourning, Son of my right hand -
Happy are those who mourn for they will be comforted, they
will understand the righteous will of God for Love to become
whole in us for all our happiness and well being in Peace.
Death the last enemy to conquer.
YHWH 'I will prove to be what I prove to be': Love
There is only Oneness with Love
There is only One Love.

****

Jasper Judah Courage	Sapphire Reuben Faith	Chalcedony Gad Happiness	Emerald Asher Peace	Sardonyx Naphtali Wrestlings to understand	Sardius Manasseh Forgive	Chrysolite Simeon Hear	Beryl Levi Adherence	Topaz Issachar Reward	Chrysoprase Zebulun Tolerance	Hyacinth Joseph Trust	Amethyst Ben Truth
Sapphire Reuben Faith	Chalcedony Gad Happiness	Emerald Asher Peace	Sardonyx Naphtali Wrestlings to understand	Sardius Manasseh Forgive	Chrysolite Simeon Hear	Beryl Levi Adherence	Topaz Issachar Reward	Chrysoprase Zebulun Tolerance	Hyacinth Joseph Trust	Amethyst Ben Truth	Jasper Judah Courage
Chalcedony Gad Happiness	Emerald Asher Peace	Sardonyx Naphtali Wrestlings to understand	Sardius Manasseh Forgive	Chrysolite Simeon Hear	Beryl Levi Adherence	Topaz Issachar Reward	Chrysoprase Zebulun Tolerance	Hyacinth Joseph Trust	Amethyst Ben Truth	Jasper Judah Courage	Sapphire Reuben Faith
Emerald Asher Peace	Sardonyx Naphtali Wrestlings to understand	Sardius Manasseh Forgive	Chrysolite Simeon Hear	Beryl Levi Adherence	Topaz Issachar Reward	Chrysoprase Zebulun Tolerance	Hyacinth Joseph Trust	Amethyst Ben Truth	Jasper Judah Courage	Sapphire Reuben Faith	Chalcedony Gad Happiness
Sardonyx Naphtali Wrestlings to understand	Sardius Manasseh Forgive	Chrysolite Simeon Hear	Beryl Levi Adherence	Topaz Issachar Reward	Chrysoprase Zebulun Tolerance	Hyacinth Joseph Trust	Amethyst Ben Truth	Jasper Judah Courage	Sapphire Reuben Faith	Chalcedony Gad Happiness	Emerald Asher Peace
Sardius Manasseh Forgive	Chrysolite Simeon Hear	Beryl Levi Adherence	Topaz Issachar Reward	Chrysoprase Zebulun Tolerance	Hyacinth Joseph Trust	Amethyst Ben Truth	Jasper Judah Courage	Sapphire Reuben Faith	Chalcedony Gad Happiness	Emerald Asher Peace	Sardonyx Naphtali Wrestlings to understand
Chrysolite Simeon Hear	Beryl Levi Adherence	Topaz Issachar Reward	Chrysoprase Zebulun Tolerance	Hyacinth Joseph Trust	Amethyst Ben Truth	Jasper Judah Courage	Sapphire Reuben Faith	Chalcedony Gad Happiness	Emerald Asher Peace	Sardonyx Naphtali Wrestlings to understand	Sardius Manasseh Forgive
Beryl Levi Adherence	Topaz Issachar Reward	Chrysoprase Zebulun Tolerance	Hyacinth Joseph Trust	Amethyst Ben Truth	Jasper Judah Courage	Sapphire Reuben Faith	Chalcedony Gad Happiness	Sardonyx Naphtali Wrestlings to understand	Sardius Manasseh Forgive	Chrysolite Simeon Hear	Beryl Levi Adherence
Topaz Issachar Reward	Chrysoprase Zebulun Tolerance	Hyacinth Joseph Trust	Amethyst Ben Truth	Sapphire Reuben Faith	Chalcedony Gad Happiness	Emerald Asher Peace	Sardonyx Naphtali Wrestlings to understand	Sardius Manasseh Forgive	Chrysolite Simeon Hear	Beryl Levi Adherence	Topaz Issachar Reward
Chrysoprase Zebulun Tolerance	Hyacinth Joseph Trust	Amethyst Ben Truth	Sapphire Reuben Faith	Chalcedony Gad Happiness	Emerald Asher Peace	Sardonyx Naphtali Wrestlings to understand	Sardius Manasseh Forgive	Chrysolite Simeon Hear	Beryl Levi Adherence	Topaz Issachar Reward	Chrysoprase Zebulun Tolerance
Hyacinth Joseph Trust	Amethyst Ben Truth	Jasper Judah Courage	Sapphire Reuben Faith	Chalcedony Gad Happiness	Emerald Asher Peace	Sardonyx Naphtali Wrestlings to understand	Sardius Manasseh Forgive	Chrysolite Simeon Hear	Beryl Levi Adherence	Topaz Issachar Reward	Chrysoprase Zebulun Tolerance
Amethyst Ben Truth	Jasper Judah Courage	Sapphire Reuben Faith	Chalcedony Gad Happiness	Emerald Asher Peace	Sardonyx Naphtali Wrestlings to understand	Sardius Manasseh Forgive	Chrysolite Simeon Hear	Beryl Levi Adherence	Topaz Issachar Reward	Chrysoprase Zebulun Tolerance	Hyacinth Joseph Trust

****

112

I wonder in these 'Enddays' of 2017/18 and a resurrection of God's spirit of Love does God's perfect love accommodate Ishmael's return to the tribe, the family of Love as a lost son returned, a family healing for oneness through Love restored for communion and unity thorough whole Love for peace to prevail? **Ishmael**'s name means 'He who listens to God' and Allah is the Arabic name for 'there is only One'. There most certainly was not perfection in Love in the Abraham, Hagar, Sarah situation, but there is much obedience to God in both sets of descendants of Abraham and fruits of the spirit evident in Christians and Muslims. It is 'by their fruits we will know them' and there is 'no division' with God's Love made complete and whole. 1st Corinthians 10-13. Perhaps an area to examine in the resurrection for peace to prevail and unity to be achieved. As it says in one psalm we can see God in the brightness of the eyes and it is clear to see who has bright eyes or not. Bright eyes are a good sign of clean mind and health and well being.

All of these states of being are what are required for Love to be made whole and positive for Love to exist and prevail. Love that is positive requires honor, joy, happiness, fun, faith, forgiveness, loyalty, commitment, tolerance and patience. We all have wrestling's with temptations in life and this is a matter of choice. If we can abide by altruistic positive choices, then we are rewarded with fulfillment in us by peace and communion of spirit. The very things in life we are all seeking, Positive sustainable Love for all. This is attainable and this can be real if we can adhere to the requirements in all our thoughts and deeds.

****

Grief and Healing

We can only find healing for our positive spirit of Love to remain in us by mourning our grievances. The obvious grief is loss through death of loved ones. But there are numerous causes of loss of our positive spirit. Emotional hurts cause grief and grievances cause us to lose our faith and become negative and lose the 'Positive Love'. When a person is not treated with faith in a positive outcome then fear and insecurity prevail. If a person's learning experience is negative, then it is hard to have positive hope and believe in the good prevailing. This is why good family values and communities are needed for the foundation of a safer and more secure, connected and loving world. Family values need to be upheld for the sake of our own humanity being able to thrive and blossom for a positive and peaceful future for the next generations.

I have worked extensively with Jonathon Bowlby's model on grief and how the grieving process is a process that needs expression and acknowledgement for processing and healing. This model has 4 distinctive phases.

1. Initial shock and numbness with a difficulty to focus and concentrate.
2. Yearning and searching with the potential for feelings of guilt and anger, meaning of life.
3. Disorientation and disorganization which can be accompanied by depression.
4. Reorganisation and resolution being able to emerge from the depression in a positive way.

I have used this model extensively in my practice and as a form of counseling for a variety of ailments. I think what is particularly powerful here is the knowing that by addressing and moving through the hurtful and painful emotions that the positive emotional cascade will occur with the emotional acknowledgement and processing.

As Jesus said in his Sermon on the Mount

'Blessed or happy are those who mourn for they will be comforted.'

It is how our bodies have been made. It is how our bodies have been made by our creator for emotional processing for healing and to restore appositive spirit of Love. In the case of grief ' death is the last enemy to conquer' because it is only the resurrection hope that can restore the spirit of Love back to the whole for a resurrection of the spirit for joy in life again. It is a perfect thought pattern for restoration of spirit in us.

****

I think this belief is faith in action as a psychological process in that if we can trust enough to let go and allow the expression of process of crying or whatever the underlying painful emotion is, then the process of acknowledgement and understanding and recognition allows the message of the emotion to be received and heard thereby it no longer serving a purpose of existence. Once the message is heard and acknowledged then the negative hurt dissipates allowing the positive emotions to prevail. This is an area that I have personally studied extensively with the belief that we as human beings are designed to be emotionally positive and happy.

My poem Lost Loves is the therapeutic process in a poem. In this poem I take you to the harsh realities of the pain of grief in order to allow a release for processing. It is not a one time read but a poem to go back to at times of need for processing. The bible says 'the last enemy' is death and death and loss of loved ones are the hardest experience in life to recover from.
But with conscious processing and a positive mindset of faith, the resurrection hope is perfect for recovering our joy in life and remembering our loved ones in our heart without the grief or pain.

****

This is the grieving process in a poem. Lost Loves is best read repeatedly and different feelings will arise with each reading so just allow and acknowledge what they are. It is ok to cry if you need to. Keep in mind the resurrection hope of seeing a loved one again. Whether in heaven or nirvana, in our hearts, in another person, does it matter where or when? We can only know what is here now in the present and if we can see them positively in our minds eye, we can remember them fondly in our hearts. It is then the loss can be accepted with grace and love. I wrote this poem after my dad died. 'Happy are those who mourn, for they will be comforted.' Matthew 5:4

****

Lost Loves

She's gone, he's gone, loved ones…
Mum, Dad, Grandparents, Children, Pets, our loved ones…
passed away, moved on to another world, another dimension,
sleeping.

Life lost at six thirty. They had been ill, popping pills for some time;
Suffering. It was expected.
No, they hadn't been ill, they had been well, healthy and a sudden
accident, heart attack, aneurism, stroke....
Stole them away from you.

Expected or unexpected, whenever it happens your world is turned
upside down, inside out suddenly changing forever.

The stillness of death is deathly quiet
like the world has stopped turning for a little while.
A peaceful, respectful, surreal still space
of bewilderment and numbness
where the birds sing a little louder than you have
ever heard them sing before.
The suns light is a little darker,
somewhat distant in the twilight
strangely beautiful in its serenity
but devastating in the circumstances
because time stops for a while
when a loved one dies.

The comprehension doesn't compute.
You know, but you don't want to know
they have gone; left.

You look for them in moments of everyday
thinking they will be back soon.
You wake up in the morning and in that instant
they are there, until the next moment
when you realize they are not there
they are gone.

Loss and loneliness adorn you
an aching in your heart
disbelief, denial and devastation
merge with fears and endless thoughts;

It shouldn't have happened like that,
If only! I should have, I shouldn't have...
At least the suffering has gone,
there is no pain now, for the dead one.

The funeral arrangements have to be made
reluctantly, busily, manically perfectly, dutifully.
How can you think what sandwich
when you can hardly eat?
The coffin, the church or crematorium
the hymns, the flowers, or not.

However, whatever, the message must be perfect.

Going through the motions
the black clothes take you to where you don't want to go.

Is this really happening?
Time is so slow:
waiting for the coffin
the inevitable about to happen
No, No, No, with disbelief,
the eyes avert.

What a valuable life valued
loved by their families
despite some difficulties,
some estranged and lonely
almost forgotten
but not quite as there is
still some love and pain there.

The Resurrection Hope, 'Jesus died for us';

for forgiveness of our sins and
He rose again from the dead
'death the last enemy to conquer'
the hardest, as death takes away life,
not only of the deceased.

It is so hard to get back the joy
and laughter in your life,
but you can, The Resurrection Hope is perfect
for life after death;
Life after death in Heaven or Nirvana?
Asleep for eternity?
Energy, chi merging with the source;
who knows?
But perfect for life on earth.
The hope that you will see them again
means they haven't really gone very far,
they are just on holiday
for a little longer than a week or two
they are still with you
in your heart and thoughts and mind;
in your cells.

They can never be taken away
if we keep them alive in us.
Their loves and values; qualities we loved
a parent's love bound by love
Still.
Love never leaves supporting, encouraging, constant.

Angers felt and injustices forgiven
words said and words that were, unsaid.
disasters mourned
for what they could have been,
should have been.
Confused feelings, repressed feelings,
feelings denied
feelings that couldn't be expressed
Loves unfulfilled, never to be.

But life and love and joy are for here;
here on earth, now;
Now and for the rest of our days
to value what and who we have
in the here and now; the present;
to have and to hold alive and living
enjoying the gift the dead have lost,

We must mourn, we must cry,
it is as He has designed us to heal.

You think you will cry forever and ever
then one day there is some comfort
and after some more tears
some more comfort
some less painful memories
and then more tears and memories
until they become happy fond memories
with no pain or tears, but a part of you.

It takes time, it is a process for completeness
and a healing for You, for us.

Jesus says 'Happy and blessed are those who mourn for they will be comforted.'

Life is the gift for the living to enjoy each and every day,
honour and value the miracle of life now and here today;

Today is our present, and it is a present only if and when we are present and it should be pleasant, Life is His gift, His presence of Love fulfilled in us.

****

Sad Tears

For when sometimes, it is hard to cry.

The mouth curved downward
like a tilted crescent moon
quivering;

Eyes searching for a safe place to
anchor trying not to let loose
the damned flood waters bulging.

The hurts, the pain wanting to explode
needing to explode via a tiny duct;

Who could imagine the deluge;
so much flood water flowing
and flowing and flowing
for healing.

As Jesus said
'Blessed are those who mourn for they will be comforted'
Matthew 5:4

****

122

There are many great thought leaders who also have similar beliefs i.e. Aristotle, the Dalai Lama, Gandhi, Buddha, Muhammad (pbuh), the Jews, and all the great prophets of the world including the scriptural teachings of Jesus Christ, 'happy are those who mourn, for they will be comforted' is true and I think that they are all teaching us the same things and that ultimately we need to overcome our differences and stresses, pain and fears in order for the emotionally positive cascades of endorphins to occur allowing Positive Love to prevail. I think that unity and oneness, unconditional love all come from this emotional and psychological profile of Love made whole and embodied in us. If peace and Love with harmony are the outcome then this is truth by spirit restored.

We can only attain to Positive Love and Positive Life by processing our inner hurts and pains and find relief through understanding and repentance and forgiveness. This in turn removes the blocks and releases energy for our own wellbeing which then affects others who we live and work with. We have to face our own truths and reality, whatever they may be. There is always a way back to Positive Love and Positive Life with Love and Faith. This is what is real and where we can find peace. We cannot find peace in fear and stress and cortisols, we need to transform out blood back to endorphins for healing to occur. Love is not a cortisol.

****

The importance of the state of the blood is critically important to well being and there are laws in scripture regarding blood. I do not think the answer to health is to allow abuse of our own bodies and to pollute our environment and then to use other peoples blood to try and treat the malfunctions of bodies that arises from toxicity of mind, body and spirit. When the body can attain to Love it has discernment at every level and it is able to process energy information for detoxification for health at every level. Well being and health and vitality is all about discernment not only at a conscious and behavioral level between good and bad, right and wrong, halal or haram but also at a cellular level of nutrient or toxin in the body. Our bodies are the temple for the spirit of Love to reside in us and the spirit of Love cannot reside with toxicity. Our internal organs can work to attain to endorphin love or they can be kept busy with detoxification for survival. They cannot do both at the same time, this is an impossible function.

I have worked with the Health Kinesiology symbiotic energy transformation (SET) procedure countless times for helping teach the body to discern toxins for detoxification and a restoration for well being. It is an amazing process and very powerful healing technique.

Isaiah 9:6 describes Jesus Christ – The Messiah, The Anointed One as a wonderful counselor and Prince of Peace. I think His consciousness certainly attains to these titles for restoring Love to be made whole in us which does make him worthy of honour and praise because only His Love heals us.

****

A **Conscious Healing Process**

Here is a process for releasing hurts and restoring Positive Love and Faith. If you have a serious problem then do seek professional help and support to help you with this process.

Identify the problem or pain.

1. Scale; no pain 1 2 3 4 5 6 7 8 9 10 agony.
2. What is it?
3. Where does it hurt?
4. Where did it come from?
5. When, how long ago?
6. Why?
7. Who?
8. What is it telling you?
9. What is it saying?
10. Where does it fit in the model of Positive Love Life Cycle?
11. Was it ultimately positive and helpful?
12. Or is it negative?
13. How is it negative and hurtful?
14. What colour is it?
15. What shape is it?
16. What can you do that is beneficial to relieve the pain for you?
17. Will you listen and nourish yourself as well as others?
18. Can you see the pain does not come from Positive Love?
19. Can you forgive or repent?

****

20. Can you let go and release for healing your spirit for Positive Love and Life?

21. Can you see you have a choice?

22. Can you see this is going to help you?

23. Can you see this will help others too?

24. Will you let go for feeling better yourself?

25. What colour is it now?

26. What shape is it now?

27. How has it changed?

28. Has it gone?

29. How do you feel now?

30. Repeat as necessary until reduced or gone.

Always seek professional help from your medical GP or health advisor.

Reasoning Love

Love is the reason. The reason we live, the reason we survive
the reason we use to reason because only Love is reasonable.

Love is why. Love is why we know right from wrong
wrong from right, haram from halal; Love is why we know.

We know. We know what is wrong and we know what is right.
We know because we feel.

We feel good or not good. Good or bad, strong or weak
happy or sad, hope or despair; confusion;

We know what we feel.

We feel positive or negative, hope or faith or fear.
Positive, faithful, happy on course or negative, fearful and
frightened,

Stressed: A Mess: Messed up.

No Love in stress and no Love in fear, because stress is not Love,
Anxiety is not Love, betrayal is not Love. Love is not a cortisol.

Love is reasonable; it will reason the wrongs with itself,
Love will ask why?

Who, where, what, when? Who Doctor? Doctor who, why?
Love is the Doctor making conscious.

Conscious of the hurt, the pain the injustice, the loss of peace, the
loss of Love, Love is the Doctor making conscious.

Consciousness for confiding, making conscious the wrong to put
right for consciousness
self conscious for understanding confidence in Love and self
actualization;

****

Reasoning; understanding the reason to be able to heal by prescribing Love for Love for Love to become Love to become whole Love in a Positive spirit

Spirits combined and doubled as Ephraim, Jerusalem becoming whole, whole as One Love;

One being who is whole, fulfilled with spirit of joy enthused with patience, kindness, peace, Love, joy, faith;

Faith in Love, faith with Love, faith that Love will become for wholeness in us that is Love for sharing,

Faith that Love will become whole and One

No fragments detached or broken by short changing Love with adrenalin, Love is not a cortisol.

Love is the beginning , the middle and the end,
The Alpha and Omega

Love is the end point, the endorphin, Love is The Point
 otherwise there is no point, no reason;

Love is the reason. Love is the only reason, the endpoint of Love;

'To be or not to be' Love, that *is* the question

Love *is* the reason, the reason *is* Love.

Chapter 11

The New Jerusalem: Two Fold Peace. Peace Above and Peace Below, Peace within ourselves and Peace with others; Heaven on Earth

Jerusalem means two fold Peace. Love made positive and whole creates two fold Peace; Peace in ourselves and Peace with others thereby Peace for others.

Jesus said if the knowledge and faith was not found on the earth when he came again then the rocks and stones would start to sing. Could this be their song?

In Revelation 21 The Holy City - New Jerusalem is defined by gemstones. Gemstones are made up of elements and so are we, in fact our whole universe is made up of elements. They originate in the stars and are the basis of everything; they are the chemistry that is the foundations of all life. Elements create gases, metals, solids, colour, they create everything.

Gemstones and their elements are significant to us in that they affect our bodily functions and they can be effective in a homeopathic fashion when they are worn on the body. Some work towards positive states of health and wellbeing, towards love and life. Others work toward atrophy and decay, degeneration, death and disintegration. This process of cell atrophy and renewal is vital for life and health and well being.

If we cultivate Love and life we can be happy and joyful and switch on our healthy cell mechanisms for life.

****

If we are not working towards a Positive state of Love in our bodies we are automatically in stress and survival with the body reacting and coping for survival. The body cannot sustain health in this stressful state of being and will make mistakes, it will become ill and lose energy, health and wellbeing leading to atrophy, degeneration and eventually death.

Many gemstones are quartz structures and quartz has the ability to hold and transmit vibration frequencies. This includes frequencies of emotion. In summary the gemstones of The Holy City; New Jerusalem and their therapeutic qualities are;

1st foundation stone = Jasper

Jasper has layers that enhance the senses which increase learning which gives protection by knowledge, discernment, sorting, understanding, satisfaction and contentment.

2nd foundation stone = Sapphire

Sapphire is a gem of faith, loyalty, love, direction, clarity and communication, hope, strength, purpose, direction and focus.

3rd foundation stone = Chalcedony

Chalcedony soothes irritations emotional and physical, spirit overcomes fleshly reactions, brings balance, happiness, joy, suppleness, flexibility and strength.

4th foundation stone = Emerald

Emerald is peace, wisdom, understanding, emotions balanced, stable, compassionate, kind, loving.

5th foundation stone = Sardonyx

Sardonyx is happy, joyous soothes irritations, spirit conquers the fleshly traits, balance, flexibility, right choice, righteousness, willing to learn, enthusiastic, positive and vitality.

6th foundation stone = Sardius

Sardius is happy, joyous, soothes irritations, balance, flexibility, spirit conquers flesh, right choices, righteousness, willingness, enthusiasm, vitality and positive.

7th foundation stone = Chrysolite

Chrysolite is a stone to reveal the truth, cast out evil, balance the mind and seek righteousness, gladdens the heart with hope.

8th foundation stone = Beryl

Beryl has Emerald qualities of wisdom, peace, knowledge, discernment, awareness, self-control, righteousness, making the right choices and is positive.

9th foundation stone = Topaz

Topaz is calming, secure, supportive, comforting, helps promote peace. Protects against envy, jealousy, covertness, the emotional motive behind destruction, sin, the challenge can we overcome and control our responses.

****

10th foundation = Chrysoprase

Chrysoprase is joy, happiness, contentment, righteousness and the qualities of a positive spirit.

11th foundation stone = Hyacinth

Hyacinth colour is often blue and helps communication, openness, honesty and integrity, knowing right from wrong and acting accordingly, loyalty, peace.

12 foundation stone = Amethyst

Amethyst is truth, calm, knowledgeable, refined, purified, regenerated, organized and content, firm secure and happy.

Jasper Judah Courage	Sapphire Reuben Faith	Chalcedony Gad Happiness	Emerald Asher Peace	Sardonyx Naphtali Wrestlings understand	Sardius Manasseh Forgive	Chrysolite Simeon Hear	Beryl Levi Adherence	Topaz Issachar Reward	Chrysoprase Zebulun Tolerance	Hyacinth Joseph Trust	Amethyst Ben Truth
Sapphire Reuben Faith	Chalcedony Gad Happiness	Emerald Asher Peace	Sardonyx Naphtali Wrestlings understand	Sardius Manasseh Forgive	Chrysolite Simeon Hear	Beryl Levi Adherence	Topaz Issachar Reward	Chrysoprase Zebulun Tolerance	Hyacinth Joseph Trust	Amethyst Ben Truth	Jasper Judah Courage
Chalcedony Gad Happiness	Emerald Asher Peace	Sardonyx Naphtali Wrestlings understand	Sardius Manasseh Forgive	Chrysolite Simeon Hear	Beryl Levi Adherence	Topaz Issachar Reward	Chrysoprase Zebulun Tolerance	Hyacinth Joseph Trust	Amethyst Ben Truth	Jasper Judah Courage	Sapphire Reuben Faith
Emerald Asher Peace	Sardonyx Naphtali Wrestlings understand	Sardius Manasseh Forgive	Chrysolite Simeon Hear	Beryl Levi Adherence	Topaz Issachar Reward	Chrysoprase Zebulun Tolerance	Hyacinth Joseph Trust	Amethyst Ben Truth	Jasper Judah Courage	Sapphire Reuben Faith	Chalcedony Gad Happiness
Sardonyx Naphtali Wrestlings understand	Sardius Manasseh Forgive	Chrysolite Simeon Hear	Beryl Levi Adherence	Topaz Issachar Reward	Chrysoprase Zebulun Tolerance	Hyacinth Joseph Trust	Amethyst Ben Truth	Jasper Judah Courage	Sapphire Reuben Faith	Chalcedony Gad Happiness	Emerald Asher Peace
Sardius Manasseh Forgive	Chrysolite Simeon Hear	Beryl Levi Adherence	Topaz Issachar Reward	Chrysoprase Zebulun Tolerance	Hyacinth Joseph Trust	Amethyst Ben Truth	Jasper Judah Courage	Sapphire Reuben Faith	Chalcedony Gad Happiness	Emerald Asher Peace	Sardonyx Naphtali Wrestlings understand
Chrysolite Simeon Hear	Beryl Levi Adherence	Topaz Issachar Reward	Chrysoprase Zebulun Tolerance	Hyacinth Joseph Trust	Amethyst Ben Truth	Jasper Judah Courage	Sapphire Reuben Faith	Chalcedony Gad Happiness	Emerald Asher Peace	Sardonyx Naphtali Wrestlings understand	Sardius Manasseh Forgive
Beryl Levi Adherence	Topaz Issachar Reward	Chrysoprase Zebulun Tolerance	Hyacinth Joseph Trust	Amethyst Ben Truth	Jasper Judah Courage	Sapphire Reuben Faith	Chalcedony Gad Happiness	Emerald Asher Peace	Sardonyx Naphtali Wrestlings understand	Sardius Manasseh Forgive	Chrysolite Simeon Hear
Topaz Issachar Reward	Chrysoprase Zebulun Tolerance	Hyacinth Joseph Trust	Amethyst Ben Truth	Jasper Judah Courage	Sapphire Reuben Faith	Chalcedony Gad Happiness	Emerald Asher Peace	Sardonyx Naphtali Wrestlings to understand	Sardius Manasseh Forgive	Chrysolite Simeon Hear	Beryl Levi Adherence
Chrysoprase Zebulun Tolerance	Hyacinth Joseph Trust	Amethyst Ben Truth	Jasper Judah Courage	Sapphire Reuben Faith	Chalcedony Gad Happiness	Emerald Asher Peace	Sardonyx Naphtali Wrestlings to understand	Sardius Manasseh Forgive	Chrysolite Simeon Hear	Beryl Levi Adherence	Topaz Issachar Reward
Hyacinth Joseph Trust	Amethyst Ben Truth	Jasper Judah Courage	Sapphire Reuben Faith	Chalcedony Gad Happiness	Emerald Asher Peace	Sardonyx Naphtali Wrestlings to understand	Sardius Manasseh Forgive	Chrysolite Simeon Hear	Beryl Levi Adherence	Topaz Issachar Reward	Chrysoprase Zebulun Tolerance
Amethyst Ben Truth	Jasper Judah Courage	Sapphire Reuben Faith	Chalcedony Gad Happiness	Emerald Asher Peace	Sardonyx Naphtali Wrestlings to understand	Sardius Manasseh Forgive	Chrysolite Simeon Hear	Beryl Levi Adherence	Topaz Issachar Reward	Chrysoprase Zebulun Tolerance	Hyacinth Joseph Trust

****

133

1 = willingness to learn, to seek 2 = belief in something better, faith 3 = ability to realize, to manifest, 4 = understanding the differences 5 = happiness, joy, flexibility, know what is right 6 = happy, understanding 7 = clarity 8 = understanding 9 = supporting 10 = joy, happiness 11 = discernment = 12 = consciousness of love, understanding love = with God.

Understanding, awareness of the differences between spirit and flesh. The ability to discern the difference and act accordingly, righteously in the accurate knowledge of Love, of God. Happiness is from a positive state of being Love, whom some call God.

All are cultivating fruitage of the spirit – Love, Joy, Peace, Long Suffering, Patience, Kindness, Goodness, Faith, Mildness, Self-Control (not to sin) for two fold Peace. The fruitage of the spirit equates to truth, trust and security for happiness and the fruits are beneficial to us.

The stones cited in the Holy City of New Jerusalem above clearly show they do reflect the qualities of Gods spirit, the spirit of Positive Love.

When we can understand what all of this means and how it is relevant to us, how it is relevant to us creating a better world where we can all be happy and healthy living in a beautiful paradise on Earth then we can receive the advice and disciplines needed to create the Positive Love. To remain in Positive Love we need to avoid fear. The only fear we should cultivate is fear of not creating a positive state of Love made whole because this enters us into negativity, fear and stress response which deplete Love, faith and happiness.

Proverbs 2:1,5 My son, if you will receive my sayings and treasure up my own commandments with yourself, in that case you will understand the fear of God, the force who causes to become.

The fear of God is the excitement of life. The eager expectation of the good, the joy attained by adhering to The Grand Creators instructions, laws of life. This positive hope is from God, from Positive Love that causes itself to become. Hope is the only positive left when everything else is negative.
The Light in the darkness.

The force for the expectation of good.

Are "The Pearly Gates" the irritations that test our faith in His Love to allow us to be in the Positive flow of energy and vitality for a Positive Life? The river of Golden Positive Energy in us for Positive Love and Positive Life where paradise can exist on Earth in us if and only if we can conquer the fears in us.

Is this the way to Peace on earth?

****

For peace and Positive Love we must remain in the Para Sympathetic Nervous System. For this we need to keep our blood sugars stable with regular nutritious wholesome foods and complete proteins. We need minerals for a health and wellbeing and especially for hormones and protein functions and electrical activity in the cell.

One important mineral I will mention here is Sulphur because according to scripture the second death occurs in 'the lake of sulphur'. Sulphur is an electrolyte needed to stabilize the shape of proteins in the body including insulin. Insulin directly affects the blood which has to maintain blood sugar and insulin levels for all body functions. In homeopathy Sulphur is known to be a remedy for all the sickness in man as the image of all sickness seems to be contained in it. Sulphur is important for detoxification and it is important for the structure of proteins which make up the body. If we cannot process the sulphur then most other body functions will be affected by this and a loss of health and vitality and energy will occur. We are made up of about 25% Sulphur.

Discernment for stability and balance on all levels;

spiritual, psychological, emotional and physical is essential for health.

****

Chapter 12

The Significance of Twelve: 12

Twelve is a very significant number. It prevails in the scriptures as Jacobs 12 sons of Israel, the 12 apostles, the women arrayed with 12 stars, the measurements of the New Jerusalem, 12 gates, 12 angels as 12 tribes, 12 apostles, and 12,000 furlongs square. Why and what is the significance? How does it relate to us and where does the 'Kingdom of Love' fit in? To find the significance of 12 I have analysed the form of the numbers; 0,1,2,3,4,5,6,7,8,9,10,11,12, 40, 144,000.

0 = whole, complete, eternal, infinite, without beginning or end.

1 = self, I, one, 1, Oneness, complete, **Love**.

2 = more than one, Heaven and Earth, spirit and flesh, self and others, division, 1 to 2, half, choice, trust, hope, **Faith**.

3 = incomplete, movement towards a new concept, change of thought, a new idea, faith, hope, **Discernment**.

4 = concept of ideas, acceptance of idea of higher place, maybe good, integration of ideas of good to self, made positive, spirit attained by bringing down from perfect ideas and embodying; **Righteous**.

5 = transcending the self, the I, the 1, the ego, the Nafs, with the possibility of the right way forward, but not yet whole or complete and trials of adherence to selfless Love, understanding, learning, **Conscious**.

6 = the wrong way forward – backward, self, selfish, fleshly, materialistic, totally apostate, separated from God of Love and spirit. Lower, surviving, seeking only physical pleasures or self-gratification, fleshly, unloving, opposing, unrighteous, learning through suffering, awakening, **Conscious**.

7 = is repentance, learning positive good right ways, becoming conscious, conscious of 7 negatives versus 7 positives, willing to learn and bring down from ideal ideas for Love, friendship, peace, making positive choices, exercising discernment, **Brotherly Love**.

8 = is whole, integrated mind, body and spirit, emotions and flesh in a healthy, balanced way, continuous, endless, 2 becoming 1, united and balanced, a positive flow, eternal, united, **Unity**.

9 = spiritual completion, mental regulation achieved, spirit realized, learned, understood, joyous, **Communion** with Love and Light, Oneness wholeness, Light, enlightened.

10 = man made whole, united with Love, Light, energy, goodness, kindness, confidence, Love made, whole, holy with self and others, **Unity**.

11 = friendship between others, confidence in self and others, self control, self actualisation with Love to others and self and God, The Golden Rule, two fold peace within and without.

12 = man united with good, holy, whole realizing difference between spirit and flesh, Heaven and Earth. Conscious. A trained conscience and ability to discern with others whilst remaining in a complete positive spirit of Love made whole.

On this basis **666** = separated from true Love of God, separated from God, negative, self-orientated, incomplete, lacking, excessive desiring in mind, emotions and flesh, never satisfied, greedy, lacking spirit, totally separate and unhappy, unfulfilled. Not whole, feeling a hole, a void, dark, self imploding, unrighteous.

77 = repentance until complete in mind & emotions = physical healing.

****

000 = whole in mind, body and spirit, in thought, word and deed.

On this basis **144,000** = man as one with Love, Light and energy, vitality, life with God's Love embodied mentally, emotionally and physically in control of desires thereby the whole spirit of Love attained. The twelve qualities of spirit squared to make whole with accurate knowledge of Love to make Love whole in us; anointed with the blood of Jesus Christ, the naturally occurring endorphin blood that comes from living in accord with God's altruistic Love made whole in us being able to attain to bliss, rapture, Heaven on Earth, 'thy will being done (in us) on Earth as in Heaven.'

40 = righteous, good incorporated consciously, mentally, physically, emotionally = attaining to a whole spirit.

The seven deadly sins are things that take away the spirit of Positive Love. Gluttony, greed, lust, sloth, wrath, envy and pride along with the 5 woes from Habakkuk which are greed, selfishness, lies, deceit and idolatry. All these selfish, fleshly traits activate the Autonomic Stress Response in us. All these negative states of being take away and betray the positive state of Love and they create fear and stress hormones which remove trust and hope and faith and the expectation of good.

By becoming negative we become faithless and create stress and fear.

Repentance is the start of sanctification –owning up being true and responding in a positive manor and being willing to make changes. Not burying, hiding truth which becomes incongruence which is not whole therefore not true.

ne book of Revelation to John is from the consciousness of Love made whole, the whole spirit which/who is Jesus Christ, The Anointed One, the whole spirit of Love embodied. The 7 letters to the 7 congregations are calling for them to repent and put their actions right. This was a refining of where they were erring in the whole spirit, they were doing good, but not wholly attainting tot the whole spirit of Love as Jesus Christ had taught. These shortfalls are clearly visible still today in organised religion and individuals who miss the point of the teachings by being competitive and divisive and judgemental falling short of the glory and wholeness of the whole spirit of Love, they have lost the Love in the debating. Genuine repentance is the milk, the start of spirituality. Without repentance we cannot see spiritually because the conscience is activated and guilt and lies and shame and self-righteousness is active.

The letters to the seven congregations;

To Ephesus although righteous in deeds and endurance they left the love they had at first. They were asked to remember from what they had have fallen and repent.

The whole spirit of Love is reminding them of Love, they had become overly righteous and lost their compassion. The needed to remember the whole spirit of **Love**.

Smyrna endured persecution and held strong in trust, they were materially poor but spiritually rich but still had the test of faith and endurance. The needed to stay positive and keep and practice true **Faith**.

Pergamum, Thyatira was living in fear and needed faith to conquer with Love made positive and whole. Thyatira needed to repent of deep things of Satan – fornication and idolatry. Was this idolizing sex and idols as we see clearly today (2018). They needed discernment of good and bad, righteous or unrighteous, haram or halal; right or wrong with Love; **Discernment**.

Sardis were dead and insensitive and needed to repent and wake up and remember the Love which they had found. They forgot the Love they had learned and lost their compassion. They needed to remember the Love, to become **Conscious**.

Philadelphia, Brotherly Love in a non violent and non sexual relationship, peace between men, no fighting, the key to friendship, peace, wisdom and understanding consciousness with a conscience, righteous for friendship amongst men; Peace for **Brotherly Love**.

Laodicea had become indifferent with no appreciation, no gratitude and no grace for the comforts they had, they had become materialistic and were blind to the source of their comforts. They had a need to repent and recognize the source of Positive Love, He that caused Love to become whole in us, Anointed, Love made whole in them. God who is Love made whole for Love to prevail deserves grace and gratitude, praise and honour.

Therefore the Kingdom of God's Love is tried by the 12 pearly gates of irritations and woes or sins that need to be conquered in us and by us. It requires huge self-control and is not so easy, but well worth the perseverance.

****

This is my conclusion, analysis and interpretation of how love and scriptural teachings occur in our earthly human body which is only human when we have the 'Hu' the enthusiasm for life through the whole spirit of Love enthused into us from Love made whole for Love, Joy, Faith, Goodness, Mildness, Kindness, Patience with Self control not to sin for Peace with Self and Peace with others – the fruits of the spirit against which there is no law. Galatians 5:22.

Jesus said 'By their fruits we will know them'. Matthew 7.

25th March 2018 I can see that sin is opposing the whole spirit of Love in mind, body and spirit – physiologically in our nervous system and by the hormonal state of the blood. Physiologically sin is anti to Love by creating a fear response; sin is a stress or fear response where stress hormones rage and cause chaos within and discomfort with self leading to disease. Forgiveness of sin is not for forgiveness to be able to continue to sin. Sin falls short of Love in us and we do not attain to the glory of His Love made whole in us. We lose out on the reward, the positive reward of endorphins and enter into stress and anxieties, confusion that can be a likened to a Hell – the burning fire of conscience where there is no peace. Sin is anti to Love so sin is anti to Christ: - I think sin is The Anti Christ and the time of grace is over and we have to attain to His Love made whole in us for happiness and health to be restored to reconnect man to be kind and connected to his heart and conscience, connected to himself as well as others and ultimately God, who is Love and causes Love to become whole in us.

We are wonderfully made for Love to create happiness in us and any that have this psychological and emotional profile are creating His love as whole. By the fruits of the spirit demonstrated we will know them, for all peoples and nations.

****

How do the 3 major monotheistic faiths compare with this information is perhaps the next area for research, along with all other teachings. I see spirit in many people of 'All Nations' and religions through Love and Faith demonstrated for Love, Peace, Joy, Patience, Tolerance for Self-Control, Goodness, Mildness, Kindness and Happiness for all; Whole Spirit attained to. I have friends from different religions who demonstrate the fruits of the spirit with loyalty and joy.

I also see the fleshly traits and betrayals where friendships disintegrate as a result with much hurt and pain caused. No loyalty, trust lost, joy lost and much hurt and pain caused where all lose out on the glory and peace of Love made whole for fulfillment. Jesus said 'by their fruits we will know them', and the fruits are clear to see. Patience and faith of fulfillment of God's promise of Love to come for all when we can surpass the sinful desires.

Love is a two way reciprocal state of being, in fact it is a three way – to God, others and self for twofold peace for all. This is perfection of Love and consciousness where all can thrive together. So be it, be Love and kind to all.

****

Scaffolding

Supporting the matrix
the horizontal negative **-** crossed with the vertical **+**
positively clamped in place,
nuts bolted; screwed together
forming 144,000 squares squared making
288,000 triangles of

Hope

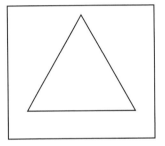

Love   Faith

The only foundations needed for building
The New Paradise for renewing Eden:
Heaven on Earth
where happiness can Positively dwell.

The Conclusion of How we Work

So how do we find Love and happiness? How can we find peace? I think it is only by knowing and practicing God's Love which is a positively conscious spiritual state of being which causes Love to become whole in us. We can use Love as a benchmark for measurement of behavior to the greater good which is the Positive force of Love which is God. To Love God, others and self means observing the requirements of the greater good, others and self for God who is Love. There is only One Love and only One God of Love who causes Love to become whole in us.

By keeping to the recommendation of love God, others and self and treating others as we like to be treated for Positive Love then the old commandments are automatically encompassed by Love and these lead to faith, 'the assured expectation of the things hoped for, the evident demonstration of realities though not beheld.' Hebrews 11. True faith is a positive belief system with belief in Positive Love with Positive outcomes for good; for a Positive Love.

Keep in truth and reality, keep awake, aware and keep conscious. Know the emotions well enough to be able to identify each one. You know and control them, not them control you. The Life Cycle (see chapter 8) can help you to discern this. Recognize fear based insecurities and exorcise them by exercising a positive state of mind over the fears and exercise the body physically.

Practice positive states of mind.

Keep true, keep in truth, only truth will set you free.

****

145

Acknowledge an error and turn around from mistakes, be sorry, say sorry, repent and forgive for trust to be established and re established for peace and Love to prevail. These behaviours give a clear conscience and peace of mind thereby creating the positive reward of endorphins that are the biochemistry for happiness, Love and faith.

Keep positively loving to all to be happy and able to reside in peace.

.

This is how the fulfillment of the New Covenant that Jesus spoke of is accomplished, The New Covenant is from the book of Jeremiah

Jeremiah 31.33 is real if it can be interpreted like this. It says

'For this is the covenant that I shall conclude with the house of Israel after those days,' is the utterance of JHVH (He who causes to Love to become). 'I will put my law within them, and in their heart I shall write it. And I will become their God, and they themselves will become my people.'34 'and they will no more teach each one his companion and each one his brother, saying, 'JHVH' for they will all of them know me, from the least one of them even to the greatest one of them, is the utterance of the force that causes Love to become whole Love. For I shall forgive their error, and their sin I shall remember no more'.

JHVH: He who causes (Love) to become whole in us by a whole spirit of Love made whole in us; Jesus Christ. Whole, complete, One, Oneness with Love, fulfillment, complete, whole, Holy.

There is only One is the meaning of the Arabic word for God; Allah and the first commandment is to have only One – because only Love is One and wholeness in us. May this universal principle of God of Love and Mercy for Peace come to be made whole in us all for a 'healing for All Nations' and a realization of our unity and Oneness through causing Love to become in each other by practicing Love to God, others and self for peace and Heaven on Earth.

Throughout our planet there are billions who exemplify fruits of the spirit (of Love) and live peacefully with one another and give generously and do not exploit others. These are the meek who will inherit the Earth. I am not sure God intended the Earth to be sold out and owned, but God has given the Earth as a provision for all to love and care and share together for everyone's benefit.

God willing in English
Insha Allah in Arabic
Shalom
Namaste

Peace and goodwill to all for a 'healing of All Nations' as promised. Revelation 21-22. Amen, Ameen, Shalom, Namaste, Peace through Love made whole in us to all.

****

Building Bridges: One Love

The ravines are deep and swirling
East and West merging new waters
emerging for rapture
fountains of peace to the world

Islam, iman, dua; peace faith and worship of Love
of Oneness in us

No divisions, no sects,   no harm, no haram, just
Halal, Hallelujah for all
freedom through Love creating trust
causing Love to become One, One whole
Holy, the whole truth and nothing but the truth

Self actualisation
seeking the pain and loss with reason
Love is the reason

La ilaha illallah, YHWH, JHVH, Yashua, Brahman, Buddha
Ohmmmmmmmmmmmmmmmmmmmmmmmmmmmmmmmmm

Is it not the meaning of the name which is truth?
Let us all become One,
Humane through One Love made whole in us
Love is always Positive.

(Inclusive of all positive belief systems not named for
'A Healing for All nations).

Note: Om the sacred sound and ohm an electrical current moving
between two points.

****

Happy and secure people who are:

Sound in mind

Stable emotionally

Energized physically

United in good attitudes and good deeds

Each individual living for the Love of the greater good who is God, for love of others and love of self

Thereby reaching their full potential as individuals and as:

Communities

Nations

Globally

Throughout the earth in peace and harmony.

Truly balanced, confident, valued, true, loved, content, happy people.

God is Love, Light, and positive energy, focused ordered, energy which is happiness to us.

Truth never changes. Truth is totally stable. Truth is reality. Truth is right.

What a perfect creation, that for our happiness and wellbeing we have to recognize, accept and practice Positive Love which does not hurt others with sin

****

It is a physical impossibility by the negative nature of the fleshly functions to be happy and secure without Positive sinless Love because it is with our minds and conscious mental regulation of faith and knowledge of Positive Love that we overcome the negative inclinations of the flesh and cast out negativity, stress and fear.

This can only be done by positively loving all and placing all fear in respect to disobeying the laws of love. Fear not placed in respect to love runs wild in us as stress, anxiety, fear, paranoia, lack of trust, loss of confidence and self worth, loss of uprightness, loss of righteousness and our humanity. Fear cages. Fear is the origin of the lie because we are not being true to our higher states of being, to our potential as humans being Love. Fear is a lie because we are not being who we are meant to be, our true self in the state of being in Love and living our truth and moral passions fully in accord with Love. It is impossible to find whole Love and trust with stress and fear because physiologically it is impossible for the two states of being to exist simultaneously in us. The lie because the potential of Love is not in being and Love is the desirable place to live as it is conscious and moral for every- ones well-being. As I say in my poem 'Reasoning Love' 'Love is not a cortisol', but an endorphin blood made from Love, trust and faith for security and peace to prevail for two fold peace which is the meaning of the name Jerusalem and the healing and pattern for making Love whole in us through all the conscious thoughts and deeds for Love as revealed through the stones cited in The Holy City, The New Jerusalem for Heaven on Earth, paradise, bliss or rapture as some call it, the promise of fulfillment of Love in us from God.
Our conscience knows everything about us and is true and does affect our behaviours.

The Whole Spirit of Love is truth with Love for forgiveness of our transgressions, to regain trust & Love, acceptance of our humanity, our uprightness as human beings, beings enthused with the whole spirit of Love, anointed with Love as is the meaning of the name Jesus Christ. This is why it is the 'most high name'.

This is what sets us apart from all other kinds and is how we are made in the image of God by emanating his qualities of Love and discernment and wow, how good is life going to be? So much positive energy we probably will not even age like we do today. Blow the ageing gene out of existence and yes the promise of everlasting life in paradise with the kingdom rule not just a hope, but a real possibility which is a reality.

The spirit of Positive Love need never die, it can be eternal, it is eternal and thus the spirit need never die with conscious understanding of how the spirit of Love is real and works in us.

Positivity only dies with negativity.
Positivity dies when we create bad which creates fear.
'Do not eat from the tree of the knowledge of good and bad for in that day you will 'positively die'. Genesis 2:16

Do you see how?
Can you see how you become negative by cultivating bad things that cause fear and anxieties and cause a stress response thus creating stress hormones?

Who knows the life of a cell and how long it replicates for? Perhaps only God who is Love and Love is eternal and everlasting. All glory and praise and thanks be to our Creator of Love, the One who causes Love to become whole in us and there is only Oneness in Love; One God.

****

151

We are designed to find happiness through Positive Love and Oneness, unity with each other by communion with Love, our creator who causes to become; who causes Love to become whole, anointed in us through His son Jesus Christ, Amen to be able to commune through whole spirit of Love with God, others and self for peace with God, others and self.

God's Love is righteous by adoption. Romans 8.15

Our will is designed to seek being happy! Our will means to seek being happy, pleased, pleasurable and joyous. Our will, desire, choices, motives, intentions attitude, principles that we live by and for fulfillment of itself as happiness is dependent on Love made whole. It is our conscience which makes us aware of our transgressions, Jesus learned through suffering as we all do, but that does not mean there is a need for suffering. Only when we know bad do we know suffering hence God's requirement in the Garden of Eden not to eat of the tree of knowledge of good and bad, because He prefers us to only know good and practice good. This is possible with a turning away from sin. Our creator has made us this way and this is far beyond any human capability however many scientists meddle with God given nature and cells.

Is our conscience the negative aspect of our will?

The conscience has to be at peace for us to truly find peace and happiness. Will is the positive application of our desires to seek Positive Love and happiness. Conscience is the will making us aware of a wrong choice. The positive will naturally seek Loves and happiness. If the desire is in accordance with Love of Love, God, others and self then Love which is God works within us and we have a sound peaceful mind. If the conscience is activated and the mind is not peaceful there is then a need to seek righteousness to find the way back to Love and happiness. This is the purpose for repentance and forgiveness as without these happiness cannot be found in a truly complete and whole way. God at work within us. Positive Love at work within us. Truth and fact!

This is what happened in the story of Adam and Eve, the conscience was activated and we have had to learn every aspect of bad in order to know good. This has taken thousands of years to do so. We are on the brink of the new world because we have regained consciousness of Positive Love which leads to Positive Life. The promised New Heavens and New Earth by positive, pure, loving, Love and Light and energy, the feel good factor sustainable and maintainable.

This is vital to our vital energy, our whole being, our life. We must listen acutely to our conscience in truth. This is what is real and where we find our answers which allow healing to occur. Finding the positive attributes. This is what is right.
It is by our positive feelings we find what is right, what is true and truth within ourselves, within us all, human beings by our outward expressions, by the spirit of good is how Love is present internally and externally. Within and without.

****

This is how we know the difference between right and wrong and can make the right, positive, choice for Love to be made whole for;

Righteousness to prevail over wrong

Good to prevail over evil

Halal over haram

God over devil

Positive + over negative –

Love to conquer sin

Trust to prevail over anxiety, fear and doubt

Peace to prevail over conflict

Righteousness to prevail for Peace and Love

Happiness, trust and security.

We have an active role in manifesting the whole spirit of Love on Earth for peace and life to exist in harmony in us. It is our responsibility. Here we will find a whole Positive Spirit of Love ruling as King of the Kingdom of Love within and without in everything, because it is only by spirit that energy moves in us. In Love, by Love, with Love. The ultimate spirit of life which is united by Love causing Love to become whole. Our will causes us to become positive or negative depending on our choices, our actions, based on Love, or not.

The creator is He who causes (Love) to become - always based on Love for Positive Love to prevail in the world. This is the law of Love so Positive Love is worthy of honour if we want to create it, Positive Love is God made whole in us; the name of Jesus Christ which, who is worthy of honour as a ruling King because He is Love made whole, anointed with Love from His Father for Oneness, wholeness in us for all our well being and there is only One.

Thanks be to The One God of Love.

Whole Love is:

Trusting
Unchangeable

Stable

Predictable

Secure

Positive

Reliable

True - Truth

This is what 'is real' the real life

Faithful and true.

Positive Love is always having a positive outcome to Positive Love, God as in the greater good, others and self. Positive Love is all encompassing. Positive Love is up building and confidence inspiring for us, for everyone, for each other. Positive Love is patient with long suffering awaiting the consciousness to evolve to understand and become positive, supporting, true, honest and inspiring for Love to prevail for peace amongst all people, all nations in accord with the promise for Heaven and Peace on Earth.

****

Do you Positively Live with trust and obedience to God, or do you become negative and doubtful demonstrating anxiety and fears to 'positively die'? The question posed at Genesis.

It is our choice, your choice. And hereby starts the discernment which affects our blood which affects our whole being and life experience.

Adam, Eve and St Agnes 'to positively die' Genesis 2:16 'neither will they learn war no more' Isaiah 2:4

Oh! what if St Agnes had been in the Garden of Eden
on that fateful day, could we be living in paradise now?
Would we be living in paradise now?
Perhaps, just, maybe...

Could we be positively living with no hurts or pain?
Just love and kindness
No jealousy, no crime, no sickness, no shame

No death of Love, no death of the Positive Spirit, no death of joy
No wars - just 'wonderful counsel': no wars - just 'Princely peace'
No wars - an 'eternal parent guiding'

What is the point of fighting? All for the same thing anyway;
that elusive prize of Positive Life; peace and love for our loved ones

'Do beat your swords into plowshares and your spears into pruning
shears' as it is written (Isaiah)

Go grow your own paradise and your own food
grow your own herbs and your own flowers,
learn grace for self control, autonomy and self worth,
heal and grow in Positive Spirit

Love each other as yourself, Love your neighbour and be kind
give love freely as   Love   takes   time.

Strong yet fragile; Sacred

One betrayal will burst Love's bubble. We become negative and
fearful; not able to trust so never betray and we can Positively Live
now. Oh St Agnes, where were you that fateful day when mankind
Positively Died?

****

Wonderfully Made

In Chinese Acupuncture the kidneys are the source of the Chi, the energy source. The kidneys discern the state of the blood and it is the adrenal glands sat above the kidney that secrete the stress hormones for when we go into a fear or stress response. When we are out of balance by being in the Sympathetic Nervous System then there is a large energy demand on other organs of the body to regulate and balance the body. This takes energy and time to process and the 5 element model demonstrates the way the energy moves in the body and the relationship between the organ functions and elements. This is used to create balance in the body and to clear blocks and restore the flow of energy for vitality. The kidneys discern to regulate the blood, endorphin love or fear, adrenaline and cortisols.

All the organ functions in the body work towards maintaining health and creating energy for regeneration and bringing balance to the body. When the body is stressed the organs have to detoxify and eliminate for survival with less energy available for the higher functions of vitality and life.

It is vitally important we respect our vital organs.

Our bodies are like bank accounts, debit or credit and the more processing work we give our body to do the harder it is to attain to Positive health with energy and vitality. Think like a hangover, we don't feel great until the body has processed all the excesses and we don't feel energized to do much. Our body forces us to stop and rest so the vital organs can clean out the excesses and any toxins. I see organ abuse on a great scale in western society trends of excessive alcohol and drug and chemical substance abuse.

****

It is the same if our immune system is fighting a germ, then our energy is being used for this vital function for survival and there will not be energy for the muscles to move freely, hence the need for rest and recuperation. The more we force our bodies through carrying on through illness, the more energy deficient problems we will see.

Contrast this with doing something we love to do where we have energy, enthusiasm, Positive Life and vitality with an abundance of life and energy enthused into us with joy.

It is simple really, common sense from using our senses and sensibility to create Positive Love, energy, Light in us. Let there be Positive Love and Light for vibrant Life for Everyone.

'Let there be Light...' So Be It... Be Love, Be Light;
Be the Light of Love.

There is only One Love that causes Love to become whole in us.

****

Light Beings: E = MC ^{2} (Albert Einstein's formula applied to our cells)

We are light beings lighted with Love
when finding our souls' passions in every delight
we are light beings sent from heaven above.

Finding our hearts' wings when white like doves
speaking our truths expelling the darkness of night
we are light beings when lighted with Love.

Saying our truths to speak of Heaven's Love
is like the sun shining, sons shining new Light
we are light beings sent from heaven above.

We are light beings ignited by Love
lighting us with light thoughts that are bright
we are light beings when lighted with Love.

Physical mass times the speed of Love
is physical mass times the speed of Light
we *can* be light beings from heaven above.

Physical mass times the speed of Love
resonates Love's energy for attaining to Light
we are light beings when lighted with Love
we are light beings sent from heaven above.

Presence

Today is our present

Our present is a present

Only if and when we are present

And it can be pleasant

Life is His gift.

A New Heaven: New Jerusalem Revelation 21

Everything real is invisible;

gifts of jasper transformed from pearls

emeralds made from sapphires squared

attaining to amethysts shining like

diamonds dancing delicately on water

chalcedony waltzing with topaz

sardonyx serenading sardius

turquoise passions speaking Love

Love being made whole like and olivine

fulfilling complete

like a mine of treasures with no dragon

no pirates or opposition

just understanding with reason

chrysolite gold molten into an emerald river

flowing to a chrysoprase sea.

****

God's Healing Love

(My interpretation from the gemstones and tribes of Israel cited in The Book of Revelation as reasoned in *Healing Poems for Positive Love, Book of Life*, and yet to be published, *Little Gems for Healing Love*, and the concepts delivered in all my poetry).

Love has courage to seek fulfillment of happiness by turning

away from sin with courage as jasper and rubies like Judah

and faith as blue as Reuben sapphires

happiness colourful as Gad and chalcedony

with the peace of Asher and emeralds

wrestlings of good and bad, haram and halal, Naphtali,

sardonyx

choices for forgiveness as Manasseh, sardius

(perhaps also forgiveness of the exiled firstborn son of Abraham,

Ishmael and a healing of the three Abrahamic faiths)

Listening, hearing as Simeon – golden chrysolite

adhering as Levi, beryl, emeralds,

Love with peace for the endorphin reward of topaz, Issachar

With the tolerance of chrysoprase, Zebulun

trust of Joseph, blue Hyacinth sapphires for faith

truth through grieving pain, mourning as Ben

for attaining the pure truth and healing

for the trust, security and peace of

amethyst Love.

'know the truth and the truth will set you free' John 8:32

****

The Therapeutic Process for Healing Love

Courage; to seek   *happiness* and fulfillment of Love; *Courage;* to repent and turn away from sin with*Faith;* in happiness and fulfillment for *peace. *Wrestlings;* with understandings – haram/ halal, good/bad right/wrong/healthy for conscious understanding to *forgive, to *Hear;* actively *listen,* empathise, understand and *adhere* too, be loyal too *Reward;* endorphin reward of Love 'just as in the twinkling of an eye' – a nervous system response with *Tolerance;* patience and *trust* in faith and love for peace via *Truth;* 'only truth can set us free' via our conscience; free from our own pains which are individual and all pain is caused by sin of some type. Truth is God's Love made whole in Oneness with self and others and God. God is Love, God causes to become, Love made whole in us, we are Love – Oneness with God and there is only One, only One Love made whole worthy of honour and praise.

Jasper Judah Courage	Sapphire Reuben Faith	Chalcedony Gad Happiness	Emerald Asher Peace	Sardonyx Naphtali Wrestlings understand	Sardius Manasseh Forgive	Chrysolite Simeon Hear	Beryl Levi Adherence	Topaz Issachar Reward	Chrysoprase Zebulun Tolerance	Hyacinth Joseph Trust	Amethyst Ben Truth
Sapphire Reuben Faith	Chalcedony Gad Happiness	Emerald Asher Peace	Sardonyx Naphtali Wrestlings understand	Sardius Manasseh Forgive	Chrysolite Simeon Hear	Beryl Levi Adherence	Topaz Issachar Reward	Chrysoprase Zebulun Tolerance	Hyacinth Joseph Trust	Amethyst Ben Truth	Jasper Judah Courage
Chalcedony Gad Happiness	Emerald Asher Peace	Sardonyx Naphtali Wrestlings understand	Sardius Manasseh Forgive	Chrysolite Simeon Hear	Beryl Levi Adherence	Topaz Issachar Reward	Chrysoprase Zebulun Tolerance	Hyacinth Joseph Trust	Amethyst Ben Truth	Jasper Judah Courage	Sapphire Reuben Faith
Emerald Asher Peace	Sardonyx Naphtali Wrestlings understand	Sardius Manasseh Forgive	Chrysolite Simeon Hear	Beryl Levi Adherence	Topaz Issachar Reward	Chrysoprase Zebulun Tolerance	Hyacinth Joseph Trust	Amethyst Ben Truth	Jasper Judah Courage	Sapphire Reuben Faith	Chalcedony Gad Happiness
Sardonyx Naphtali Wrestlings understand	Sardius Manasseh Forgive	Chrysolite Simeon Hear	Beryl Levi Adherence	Topaz Issachar Reward	Chrysoprase Zebulun Tolerance	Hyacinth Joseph Trust	Amethyst Ben Truth	Jasper Judah Courage	Sapphire Reuben Faith	Chalcedony Gad Happiness	Emerald Asher Peace
Sardius Manasseh Forgive	Chrysolite Simeon Hear	Beryl Levi Adherence	Topaz Issachar Reward	Chrysoprase Zebulun Tolerance	Hyacinth Joseph Trust	Amethyst Ben Truth	Sapphire Reuben Faith	Chalcedony Gad Happiness	Emerald Asher Peace	Sardonyx Naphtali Wrestlings understand	Sardius Manasseh Forgive
Chrysolite Simeon Hear	Beryl Levi Adherence	Topaz Issachar Reward	Chrysoprase Zebulun Tolerance	Hyacinth Joseph Trust	Amethyst Ben Truth	Sapphire Reuben Faith	Chalcedony Gad Happiness	Emerald Asher Peace	Sardonyx Naphtali Wrestlings understand	Sardius Manasseh Forgive	Chrysolite Simeon Hear
Beryl Levi Adherence	Topaz Issachar Reward	Chrysoprase Zebulun Tolerance	Hyacinth Joseph Trust	Amethyst Ben Truth	Sapphire Reuben Faith	Chalcedony Gad Happiness	Emerald Asher Peace	Sardonyx Naphtali Wrestlings to understand	Sardius Manasseh Forgive	Chrysolite Simeon Hear	Beryl Levi Adherence
Topaz Issachar Reward	Chrysoprase Zebulun Tolerance	Hyacinth Joseph Trust	Amethyst Ben Truth	Sapphire Reuben Faith	Chalcedony Gad Happiness	Emerald Asher Peace	Sardonyx Naphtali Wrestlings to understand	Sardius Manasseh Forgive	Chrysolite Simeon Hear	Beryl Levi Adherence	Topaz Issachar Reward
Chrysoprase Zebulun Tolerance	Hyacinth Joseph Trust	Amethyst Ben Truth	Sapphire Reuben Faith	Chalcedony Gad Happiness	Emerald Asher Peace	Sardonyx Naphtali Wrestlings to understand	Sardius Manasseh Forgive	Chrysolite Simeon Hear	Beryl Levi Adherence	Topaz Issachar Reward	Chrysoprase Zebulun Tolerance
Hyacinth Joseph Trust	Amethyst Ben Truth	Sapphire Reuben Faith	Chalcedony Gad Happiness	Emerald Asher Peace	Sardonyx Naphtali Wrestlings to understand	Sardius Manasseh Forgive	Chrysolite Simeon Hear	Beryl Levi Adherence	Topaz Issachar Reward	Chrysoprase Zebulun Tolerance	Hyacinth Joseph Trust
Amethyst Ben Truth	Jasper Judah Courage	Sapphire Reuben Faith	Chalcedony Gad Happiness	Emerald Asher Peace	Sardonyx Naphtali Wrestlings to understand	Sardius Manasseh Forgive	Chrysolite Simeon Hear	Beryl Levi Adherence	Topaz Issachar Reward	Chrysoprase Zebulun Tolerance	Hyacinth Joseph Trust

****

Revelation 21: New Heavens, a crystal fountain for healing pain, the re gathering of Israel: 144,000 states of being; causing love to become whole in us for resurrecting and manifesting a whole spirit of positive love worthy of honour for love and Peace on Earth.

Isaiah 9:6: 'For there has been a child born to us, there has been a son given to us, and his name will be called Wonderful Counsellor, Mighty God, Eternal Father, Prince of Peace': Love is the reason for and to heal because only love is reasonable.

Healing of pain for peace on earth through the whole spirit of love that is positive in man for kindness: + Love, Faith, Discernment, Righteous, Consciousness, Friendship, Unity, Communion. So Be It for Peace and life in Heaven and on Earth. War no more, kill no more, create the beauty in life for all... with forgiveness. So be it, be Love, to be Love is the answer, the Light of understanding reason who is One, One God who causes Love to become whole, anointed with His whole Spirit for Ephraim a double portion of Love and Peace on Earth. With God's Love made whole should there be a return and welcoming home of a lost son of Abraham? Ishmael, who's name means 'He who listens to God' for 'A Healing for All Nations'.

Amen.

God Willing in English, Insh Allah in Arabic, Shalom, Namaste, So be Love for Peace to all.

More to come very soon.
****

Revelation 21: The Holy City: New Jerusalem: Zion.

144,000 thoughts sealed for healing and creating Love made Positive and whole for the Light of understanding Love with reason for conscious enlightenment of Positive Love for Peace within and Peace without for removing pain and a 'healing of All Nations' as promised. 'I shall prove to be what I prove to be' Exodus 3:14: Love: 'God is Love' 1 John 4:8 Let Love conquer fear with God's Love made whole in us. Fear and sin activate the autonomic nervous system stress response. Sin is anti to Christ's Love, 'Love is not a cortisol', but the end: the natural endorphin release in us from loving the Love of God: 'Book of Life'. We are changed 'just as in the twinkling of an eye' 1 Corinthians 15:51-2.
The river of water of Life, clear as crystal, trees of Life producing 12 crops of fruit for the spirit to be made whole for a 'curing of the nations'. Revelation 22 'Yes. He is coming quickly. Come Lord Jesus come.'
'Nation will not lift up sword against nation neither will they learn war anymore' Isaiah 2;4
'Let thy Kingdom come on Earth as it is in Heaven' Matthew 6:5 Luke 11:1

Nothing added, nothing taken away, just translated into a visual of the universal language of consciousness of Love made whole, Holy Anointed for 'the fruits of the spirit' to become manifest namely 'Love, Joy, Faith, Patience, Kindness, Goodness, Mildness, Self Control (not to sin) for Ephraim: Two fold Peace: Jerusalem. Against such things there is no law.' Galatians 5:22, The Golden Rule 'To Love God, to Love others as self'. God is Light and Love and causes Love to become whole in us and three is only Oneness in Love, the meaning of the names of God; YHWH;JHVH, YashuaAnointed: One Love Jesus Christ manifested in us. Jesus said 'By their fruits we will know them.' The whole spirit of consciousness the apostles attained to. 'And during the arriving of the day of Pentecost they were all together in The One Place' Acts 2:1 The whole place of Love. There is no division with God's Love made whole in mind, body and spirit, the Oneness and completeness of Love; Parousia: Love's Light Revealed. The seven spirits of Love: Love (which always a positive outcome) Faith, Discernment, Righteousness, Consciousness, Brotherly Love for Unity: Communion with One Love: There is only One. Amen, Ameen, Shalom, Namaste, Peace to All Nations.

****

A Vision of the Healing Light of Love

Thanks be to God.

'Let there be Light' of Love.

I believe this is Faithfull and True

'Come Lord Jesus Come'

I see no other way.

In good Faith and Positive Love

Francess xxx.

Some Poems

Life Energy

Joy, laughter and a smile
lasting more than a little while

Aglow inside energizes a glow outside
illuminating a rainbow aura with
golden positive light flowing like the river of life
cells firing madly, communicating rapidly
switching on the processes to life;

Pure and golden white light
like an angel in the night
have no fear, only Love and we can live
with the hope from above;

All pain released, processed and forgotten
forgiven and bonded by Love for union
and unity, peace, goodwill and grace.

Contentment and fulfillment with a happy smile
make this life *so* worthwhile.

****

Sonnet for a Loving God

If God had a healing method what would it be?
Would it be based on science and chemistry?
Chemistry not of the laboratory kind
But chemistry born in the blood out of mind.

How can mind do that you may ask?
And I may say this is a complex task
A complex task this may be
To attain to thoughts that are heavenly.

It seems to me we have lost the divine
Who gives us the power to love all the time
In whom does it make a difference to create
Let me assure you there is no mistake;

Only His Love teaches wholeness of mind
Only His Love teaches gentleness for Man to be kind.

****

Poppies

Floppy poppies floating in the sun
Are a source of joy for everyone
They should grow amongst the wheat we eat
And in small doses are a treat.

Like frankincense they conquer fear
But only if we respect them dear
They help remove the pain of man
But wont fulfil the challenge or plan.

You see it is up to us to grow
Like scarlet poppies in the snow
Fighting off the frost and cold with
Loves golden, reddened glow.

When we find that golden glow
Our own opiates we can grow.

****

The End

The end is the start of the beginning of the word endorphin
the end of the quest for heart smiles in Love
mimicked by opium posing as opiates
killing pain knowing pleasure
addictive, seductive, seducing
ending enslavement to cortisols crying for an end,
the end; the release of endorphins
the dopamine, the serotonin, the oxytocin , the anandamide
binding the blood in marriage with Love
which is always positive
the endorphin is the end
the end is the beginning of The Word: Endorphin:
His Love in our blood
Freedom. The end is the beginning of The Promise;
His Promise to end pain
The End is the beginning
 'for look I am making all things new'.

Revelation 21:5

****

Crown of Stones: For You

Jasper, Sapphire, Chalcedony, Emerald, Sardonyx, Sardius,
Chrysolite, Beryl, Topaz, Chrysoprase, Hyacinth, Amethyst.

The crown of stones are;
For You
For your Love to be made whole
For You
For your pain to be healed
For You
For your heart to beat as one with Love
For You
For your thinking and feeling hemispheres to be joined
For You
For Love to conquer fear
For You, in you
For enlightenment of Love's Light
For You
For Love of God who is Love of others as self,
For You
A perfect measure made perfect; Golden;
For You
For mind, body and spirit to be One, joined, connected, whole (0);
One (1), I, (I), The' I Am'
Made whole again in Love (who is God)
In You, For You; Self Actualization, Khudi
Only Love is One, Complete, unbroken
For you
Vitality; vibrant vibrations resonating positive energy for life,
Well being and peace
For You and for Others to be made whole in God's Love again.
Thanks be to God.

****

The Heavenly City

When will she come to be?
Zion: radiant with Love's Light
gleaming with gems of consciousness
of the promised land for healing pain
for 'All Nations', for all people
for the healing of pain for peace on Earth
from Heaven
                              to Earth
two fold peace doubled as Ephraim
within and without
above and
                    below
for Heaven to come down to earth;
It is His Promise;
this city radiant with Love's Light.

Please enter freely and bathe in her light
of minerals that Linus Pauling said
'you can trace every sickness, every disease, and every ailment to a
mineral deficiency'.

Just as Sulphur in homeopathy is relevant to every disease, so it is
when Jesus Christ, The Whole Spirit of Love says through John in
The Book of Revelation that sin puts us into the fiery lake of
Sulphur;
cells debased as a six, six and a six: Sick
proteins destabilized by cortisols of doubt.

Minerals and elements holding sacred geometrical forms
turning a hexagon into an octagon
                    (as seen in many ecclesiastical tiles)
Mans' imperfection made whole
transformed to an infinite flow of eights
for perfecting the flow for Love to flow freely
as a river of Gold
Eights: upright infinities of endorphin blood
****

offering a blueprint for eternal life
of the spirit made whole with Our Fathers' Love
where spirit will not be cracked or broken but
'will reach the height of Everest' and beyond;
perhaps the true Kohinoor;
The true 'Mountain of Light'.

Amen, Ameen, Shalom, Namaste, Peace to All Nations.

Notes and Reflections

Some space for your thoughts and feelings:

What fears do you want to conquer with Love?
Where are your stresses?
What negative emotion are you holding on to?

Place your hands across your forehead and focus on the fears and observe them melt away into conscious reason and a release of their restraints on Love to allow peace and healing.

This is a constant process of re newel of the self to maintain a positive spirit and transform from persistent stress to Peace and Love.

We call this ESR – Emotional Stress Release and I learned it as part of my professional training from the Touch for Health Manual by Dr John Thie – another of my Bibles. Astounding knowledge of how our bodies connect and work for the lay person and professional.

It can also be soothing to add in one drop of an essential oil like Frankincense or Rose or Lavender or Jasmine diluted in a natural carrier oil when done at night (as long as you are not allergic and keep away from sunlight and your eyes). Also nice if a partner or friend can do for you. Sometimes there may be tears but do not hold them back for Jesus said ' Blessed/ Happy are those who mourn for they will be comforted.' Matthew 5:4

The grieving process is essential for healing the pain of loss, 'death is the last enemy'. I know this is true!

****

You could also add a crystal with consciousness in accord with The New Jerusalem aspect of Healing of course. Stress maybe work, person, grief, anger, lack of confidence, pain, tiredness, loss of energy, too much to do, conflict, jealousy, regret, envy, hatred, excess alcohol, drugs, stimulants, betrayal, divorce, loss, loss of everything, move, country culture, financial, death, abuse, violence, restrictions, control, relationship difficulties, many more things, too many to name.

****

Emotional Stress Processing Procedure

Stress - name one at a time and write how it affects your life.

....
....
....
....
....
....

Pain Level before ESR   1 2 3 4 5 6 7 8 9 10
Please circle

Pain Level after ESR   1 2 3 4 5 6 7 8 9 10
Please circle

Feelings now

....
....
....
....
....
....
....
....
....
....
....

Maybe worry has gone, more comfortable, less pain, not a problem, can cope with sorting out, more confident, happier, easier, more joy, more understanding, doesn't matter anymore. Always good to clarify and I always thank God. Please copy and share Repeat for each pain or discomfort.

****

Emotional Stress Processing Procedure

Stress - name one at a time and write how it affects your life.

....
....
....
....
....
....

Pain Level before ESR   1 2 3 4 5 6 7 8 9 10
Please circle

Pain Level after ESR   1 2 3 4 5 6 7 8 9 10
Please circle

Feelings now

....
....
....
....
....
....
....
....
....
....
....

Maybe worry has gone, more comfortable, less pain, not a problem, can cope with sorting out, more confident, happier, easier, more joy, more understanding, doesn't matter anymore. Always good to clarify and I always thank God. Please copy and share Repeat for each pain or discomfort.

****

Emotional Stress Processing Procedure

Stress - name one at a time and write how it affects your life.

....

....

....

....

....

....

Pain Level before ESR   1 2 3 4 5 6 7 8 9 10
Please circle

Pain Level after ESR   1 2 3 4 5 6 7 8 9 10
Please circle

Feelings now

....

....

....

....

....

....

....

....

....

....

....

Maybe worry has gone, more comfortable, less pain, not a problem, can cope with sorting out, more confident, happier, easier, more joy, more understanding, doesn't matter anymore. Always good to clarify and I always thank God. Please copy and share Repeat for each pain or discomfort.

***

****

Emotional Stress Processing Procedure

Stress - name one at a time and write how it affects your life.

....

....

....

....

....

....

Pain Level before ESR   1 2 3 4 5 6 7 8 9 10
Please circle

Pain Level after ESR   1 2 3 4 5 6 7 8 9 10
Please circle

Feelings now

....

....

....

....

....

....

....

....

....

....

....

Maybe worry has gone, more comfortable, less pain, not a
problem, can cope with sorting out, more confident, happier,
easier, more joy, more understanding, doesn't matter
anymore. Always good to clarify and I always thank God.
Please copy and share Repeat for each pain or discomfort.

****

Emotional Stress Processing Procedure

Stress - name one at a time and write how it affects your life.

....
....
....
....
....
....

Pain Level before ESR   1 2 3 4 5 6   7 8 9 10
Please circle

Pain Level after ESR   1 2 3 4 5 6   7 8 9 10
Please circle

Feelings now

....
....
....
....
....
....
....
....
....
....
....

Maybe worry has gone, more comfortable, less pain, not a
problem, can cope with sorting out, more confident, happier,
easier, more joy, more understanding, doesn't matter
anymore. Always good to clarify and I always thank God.
Please copy and share Repeat for each pain or discomfort.

_____

****

Emotional Stress Processing Procedure

Stress - name one at a time and write how it affects your life.

....

....

....

....

....

....

Pain Level before ESR   1 2 3 4 5 6 7 8 9 10
Please circle

Pain Level after ESR   1 2 3 4 5 6 7 8 9 10
Please circle

Feelings now

....

....

....

....

....

....

....

....

....

....

....

Maybe worry has gone, more comfortable, less pain, not a problem, can cope with sorting out, more confident, happier, easier, more joy, more understanding, doesn't matter anymore. Always good to clarify and I always thank God. Please copy and share Repeat for each pain or discomfort.

****

Emotional Stress Processing Procedure

Stress - name one at a time and write how it affects your life.

....
....
....
....
....
....

Pain Level before ESR   1 2 3 4 5 6 7 8 9 10
Please circle

Pain Level after ESR   1 2 3 4 5 6 7 8 9 10
Please circle

Feelings now

....
....
....
....
....
....
....
....
....
....
....

Maybe worry has gone, more comfortable, less pain, not a problem, can cope with sorting out, more confident, happier, easier, more joy, more understanding, doesn't matter anymore. Always good to clarify and I always thank God. Please copy and share Repeat for each pain or discomfort.

****

Notes:

****

Resources and Bibliography:

Books in my library – which will have influenced my work in some way: As a dyslexic I dip into knowledge as and when I need it. I struggle to read at any length and I learn as I need to know the understanding of something. Much of my knowledge is experiential and most of my learning has been by hands on experiences from my work. I think touch transmits energy understandings and I have the ability to translate the understandings for healing. I always had the ability to emotionally process 'stuff' or 'issues' which was an enormous blessing as I had much 'stuff' and 'issues' to sort through and even with these 'issues' I managed to transcend them. It was much later in my life I realized that the pains were originated from a lack of love, from sin and fleshly traits and that the love and healing I experienced was The Love and Light of God's healing Love. My first and foremost book on healing is The Holy Bible and my faith in Jesus Christ and the promise from God for healing has been my life and hope.

God's Love is righteous by adoption. Romans 8.15

The Holy Bible

My professional training

Books on anatomy and physiology

Books on healing and energy

Books on stress

Books on history

Geology

My Life

How I have worked out my own issues

My observations of conscious processing in my work

Understanding Love

Music

Grief

Compassion

Love

Bibliography – books in my home library which have contributed to my understandings

Abbott, J, Ryan, T, *The unfinished revolution,* Network educational press Ltd, 2000

Aeschlimann, E, D'ancona, P, *The art of illumination; An anthology of manuscripts from the sixth to the sixteenth century,* Phaidon, 1969

Alexander, D, *Rebuilding the matrix,* Lion publishing, 2001

Allegro, J.M, *The Dead sea scrolls,* Penguin books LTD, 1956

Arnould-Taylor, W.E, *Aromatherapy for the whole person,* Arnould-Taylor education LTD, 1981

Bach, R, *Jonathan Livingston Seagull; a story,* Turnstone Press, 1972

Baigent, M, Leigh, R, Lincoln, H, *The holy blood and The holy grail,* Corgi Books, 1983

Barnard, C, *50 ways to a healthy heart,* Thorsons, 2001

Bauval, R, Hancock, G, *Keeper of Genesis,* William Heinemann Ltd, 1996

Bek, L, Pullar, P, *The seven levels of healing,* Century Hutchinson Ltd, 1986

Bek, L, Wilson, A, *What colour are you? The way to health through colour,* The Aquarian Press, 1981

Berkeley, G, *Principles of human knowledge/three dialogues,* Penguin books, 1988

Bhajan, Y, *The ancient art of self- nutrition,* Khalsa Clinic, 1980

Bohatec, M, *Illuminated manuscripts,* Artia, 1970

Boteach, S, *Kosher emotions; A guided tour of the heart,* Hodder & Stoughton, 2000

Brady, K, Considine, M, *Holistic London,* Brainwave, 1990

****

Breathnach, S, *Simple abundance*, Transworld publishers, 1995

Brennan, R, *The Alexander technique workbook*, Element books limited, 1992

Briers, S, *Brilliant cognitive behavioural therapy*, Pearson education limited, 2009

Bronowski, J, *The ascent of man*, British Broadcasting Corporation, 1973

Bryce-Smith, Hodgkinson, D, L, *The Zinc solution*, Arrow books limited, 1986Chaitow, L, *Thorsons guide to Amino Acids*, Thorsons, 1991

Butler, B, *An introduction to kinesiology*, T.A.S.K. Publications, 1990

Butler, B, *Your Breasts*, T.A.S.K Books, 1993

Byers, D, *Better health with foot reflexology*, Ingham publishing, 1983

Caplin, C, *Holistix,* Sidgwick & Jackson LTD, 1990

Capra, F, *The Tao of Physics*, Wildwood House, 1975

Carr, A, *Easywegh to lose weight*, Penguin books, 1997

Carlisle, P, *The medical detective; memoirs of a most unusual doctor*, Abaco book publishing LTD, 2010

Cavendish, R, *Encyclopedia of the unexplained*, Routledge & Kegan Paul Ltd, 1974

Chaitow, L, *Vaccination and immunisation,* The C.W. Daniel Company Limited, 1987

Chancellor, P.M, *Bach flower remedies*, The C.W. Daniel company LTD, 1971

Chown, M, *Afterglow of creation,* Arrow books, 1993

Christopher, J, *Regenerative Diet,* Christopher publications, 1982

Claremont de Castillejo, I, *Knowing woman*, G.P. Putnam's sons, 1973

Clarke, S, *Essential chemistry for aromatherapy*, Elsevier Ltd, 2002

****

Clements, H, *Nature cure for shingles and cold sores*, Thorsons publishers limited, 1977

Cohen, M, *Philosophy for dummies*, John Wiley & Sons LTD, 2010

Courtenay, A, Tourelle, M, *Thorsons introductory guide to Kinesiology*, Thorsons, 1992

Cowie, I, *Jesus' healing works and ours*, Wild goose publications, 2000

Culbert, S.J, *Colourgenics as body language*, W.Foulsham & company limited, 1987

Cunningham, S, *Crystal, Gem and Metal magic*, Llewellyn Publications, 1987

Cutler, H, Lama, H, *The art of happiness*, Hodder & Stoughton, 1998

Cyriax, J, *Text-book of Orthopaedic medicine*, Cassell & Company Ltd, 1944

Davidson, J, *Subtle Energy*, The C.W. Daniel Company, 1987

Davidson, J, *The web of life,* The C.W. Daniel Company, 1988

Davies, R, *How to read faces*, Aquarian Press, 1989

Davies, S, Stewart, A, *Nutritional Medicine*, Pan Books, 1987

Davis, A, *Lets have healthy children,* The new American library, 1951

Davis, P, *Aromatherapy; An A-Z,* The C.W. Daniel Company Limited, 1988

Dennison, P, *Edu-K for Kids*, Edu-Kinethetics, 1987

Dewe, B, Dewe, J, *Professional Health Provider 1*, Professional Health practice workshops, 1990

De Bono, E, *The six value medals*, Vermillion, 2005

De Paoli, C, Elliot, R, *Kitchen Pharmacy; A book of healing remedies*, Chapmans publishers, 1991

De Vries, J, *Traditional home and herbal remedies*, Mainstream publishing company, 1986

Diamond, J, *Life energy*, Dodd, Mead & Company, 1985

Diamond, J, *Life- energy analysis: A way to cantillation*, Archaeus Press, 1988

Diamond, J, *Notes on the spiritual basis of therapy*, Archaeus Press, 1986

Diamond, J, *The life energy in music; volume 1*, Archaeus Press, 1981

Diamond, J, *The life energy in music; volume 2*, Archaeus Press, 1983

Diamond, J, *The life energy in music; volume 3*, Archaeus Press, 1986

Diamond, J, *The re-mothering experience; How to totally love*, Archaeus Press, 1981

Diamond, M, *Fit for life; A new way of eating*, Bantam, 1987

Drosnin, M, *The bible code*, Weidenfeld & Nicolson London, 1997

Dunne, L, *Nutrition Almanac; Third edition*, McGraw-Hill, 1990

Dychtwald, K, *Bodymind*, Jeremy P. Tarcher, 1977

Earle, L, *Vitamins & minerals*, Boxtree Limited, 1994

Edwards, G, *Living Magically*, Judy Piatkus, 1991

Egoscue, P, *The Egoscue method of health through motion*, HarperCollins Publishers, 1992

Emoto, M, *The hidden messages in water*, Beyond Words Publishing, 2004

Evans, P, *The verbally abusive relationship*, Adams media, 2010

Every, G, *Christian Mythology*, The Hamlyn Publishing group, 1970

Eysenck, H.J., *Psychology is about people*, The Penguin press, 1972

Finn, G, Harland, M, *Healthy Business; The natural practitioner's guide to success*, Madeline Harland & Glen Finn, 1990

Foster, H, *Eat 5*, Hamlyn, 2002

****

Fraser, Hill, R, S, *The roots of health*, Green books, 2001

Fremantle, A, *Age of faith*, Time Inc., 1965

Freud, S, 2. *New introductory lectures on psychoanalysis*, Penguin group, 1991

Gallant, A, *Body treatments and dietetics for the beauty therapist*, Stanley Thornes Ltd, 1978

Gallant, A, *Principles and techniques for the beauty specialist*, Stanley Thornes Ltd, 1975

Gawkrodger, D, *Dermatology*, Churchill Livingstone, 1992

Gimbel, T, *Healing through colour*, C.W. Daniel Company limited, 1980

Goldsworthy, G, *According to plan*, Inter-varsity Press, 1991

Greenfield, S, *Inside the body*, Cassell illustrated, 2004

Gross, R, *Psychology; The science of mind and behaviour*, Hodder & Stoughton, 1992

Grove-Stephenson, I, Quilliam, S, *The best counselling guide*, Thorsons, 1990

Hall, D, *Iridology*, Angus & Robertson publishers, 1980

Hall, J, *The Crystal Bible Vol 1*, Godsfield Press, 2003

Hamly, P, *The life and times of Leonardo*, The Hamlyn publishing group, 1965

Hancock, G, *Fingerprints of the Gods*, William Heinemann Ltd, 1995

Hanssen, M, *E for additives*, Thorsons Publishers Limited, 1984

Hardy, D, *The compound effect*, Success books, 2010

Harries, Mclatchie, , King, Williams, G, M, J, C, *ABC of sports medicine*, BMJ pubishing group, 1995

Hawking, S, *A brief history of time*, Bantam Press, 1988

****

Hay, L, *Heal your body*, Eden grove editions, 1989

Hay, L, *You can heal your life*, Eden grove editions, 1988

Heller, J, Henkin, W, *Bodywise: Regaining your natural flexibility and vitality for maximum well-being*, Jeremy P. Tarcher, 1986

Helvin, M, *Bodypure*, Headline book publishing, 1995

Hinkel, A, *Electrolysis, Thermolysis and the blend: The principles and practice of permanent hair removal,* Arroway, 1968

Hodgkinson, L, *The anti-celluite recipe book*, Grafton paperbacks, 1990

Hodgson, J, *Wisdom in the stars*, The white eagle lodge, 1943

Holdway, A, *Kinesiology*, Element books, 1995

Holford, P, *The optimum nutrition bible*, Judy Piakus publishers Ltd, 1997

Holford, P, Neil, K, *Balancing hormones naturally*, Judy Piakus publishers LTD, 1998

Horan, P, *Abundance through Reiki*, Lotus Light Publications, 1995

Howard, M, *Candle burning its occult significance*, The Aquarian press, 1975

Ironside, V, *'You'll get over it'*, Penguin Books LTD, 1996

Jeffers, S, *Feel the fear and do it anyway*, Century Hutchinson Ltd, 1987

Jenson, B, *Doctor-patient handbook*, Bernerd Jenson enterprises, 1976

Jenson, B, *The Science and Practice of Iridology*, Bernerd Jenson, 1987

Jenson, B, *Tissue cleansing through bowel management*, Bernerd Jenson, 1981

Jobe, F, *Athletic Forever*, Contemporary books, 1999

Johnson, D, *What the eye reveals; An introductions to the rapid method of Iris interpretation*, Rayid publications, 1984

Joshi, N, *Dr Joshi's holistic detox*, Hodder & Stoughton, 2005

Josiah, E, *Love; The key to enlightenment,* Able Publishing, 1999

Josiah, E, *Power and freedom; The essence of the human spirit,* Able Pubishing 1999

Kapit, Elson, W, L, *The anatomy colouring book,* Harper & Row publishers, 1977

Kaplan, M, *Crystal and gemstones: Windows of the self,* Cassandra Press, 1987

Katie, B, *A thousand names for Joy,* Rider, 2007

Keele, K.D, Poynter, F.N.L, *Science in society; A short history of medicine,* F.N.L. Poynter and K.D. Keele, 1961

Kennedy, C, *Guide to the management gurus; Shortcuts to the ideas of leading management thinkers,* Century Ltd, 1991

Kenton, L, *The Biogenic diet,* Century, 1986

Kenyon, J, *Acupressure techniques; A self-help guide,* Thorsons publishing group, 1987

Key, S, *Back in action,* Vermilion, 1993

Khan, P, *Introducing Spirituality into counselling and therapy,* Omega Publications, 1982

Kilmartin, A, *Understanding Cystitis,* Heinemann Health books, 1973

Kirsta, A, *The book of stress survival,* Unwin paperbcks, 1986

Kloss, J, *Back to eden,* Back to eden books, 1949

Kozminsky, I, *The magic and science of Jewels and Stones, Vol 1,* Cassandra Press, 1988

Kozminsky, I, *The magic and science of Jewels and Stones; Vol 2,* Cassandra Press, 1988

Krebs, C, *A revolutionary way of thinking,* Hill of content publishing, 1998

****

Kriege, T, *Fundamental basis of Irisdiagnosis*, L.N. Fowler & Co Ltd, 1969

Kushi, M, *Your face never lies*, Red moon press, 1976

Iqbal, *Sir Muhammad The Reconstruction of Religious Thought in Islam Kitab Bhevan 1974*

Lacroix, N, *Massage for total relaxation*, Dorling Kindersley limited, 199

Lazarides, L, *The nutritional health bible*, Thorsons, 1997

LeDoux, J, *The emotional brain*, Weidenfeld & Nicolson, 1998

Licauco, J, *The magicians of God*, National Book store, 1981

Lidell, L, *The book of yoga*, Ebury press, 1983

Lindlahr, H, *Philosophy of natural therapeutics*, The Maidstone Osteopathic clinic, 1975

Lipton, B, *The biology of belief*, Hay House, 2005

Livesey, R, *Understanding Alternative Medicine*, Bury House Christian books, 1983

Mackarness, R, *Not all in the mind*, Pan Books ltd, 1976

Magnusson, M, *Lindisfarne; The cradle Island,* Oriel Press, 1984

Manning, M, *Guide to self healing*, Thorsons publishers Ltd, 1989

Mansfield, P, *The good health handbook*, Grafton books, 1988

Maxwell-Hudson, C, *The book of Massage*, Ebury press, 1984

McKenna, P, *Change your life in 7 days*, Bantam press, 2004

McKenna, P, *I can make you thin*, Bantam press, 2005

McPherson, T, *Philosophy and religious belief,* Hutchinson & Co Ltd, 1974

McTaggart, L, *What doctors don't tell you*, Thorsons, 1996

****

Meadows, P, *Pressure points*, Word publishing, 1998

Mervyn, L, *The vitamins explained simply*, Newman Turner publications limited, 1985

Mervyn, L, *Thorsons complete guide to vitamins & minerals*, Thorsons publishers limited, 1986

Mindell, E, *The vitamin bible*, Arlington books Ltd, 1982

Morgan, P, *Natural remedies for allergies*, Parragon, 1998

Morris, J, *Beauty therapists handbook*, B T Batsford Limited, 1987

Nelson-Jones, R, *The theory and practice of counselling psychology*, Holt, Rainhart and Winston Ltd, 1988

Nissim, R, *Natural healing in gynecology*, Pandora press, 1986

Page, C, *Frontiers of health*, The C.W. Daniel Company Limited, 1992

Palmer, M, *The healing power of crystals,* Century Hutchinson Ltd, 1988

Peck, M, *The road less travelled*, Rider, 1978

Pert, C, *Molecules of emotion,* Scribner, 1997

Peterson, N, *Herbal Remedies*, Blitz Editions, 1995

Raphaell, K, *Crystal healing*, Aurora Press, 1987

Reece, I, Walker, S, *Teaching, Training and Learning*, Business Educators publishers Ltd, 2003

Rifenbary, J, *No Excuse!,* Success publishers, 1995

Rochlitz, S, *Allergies and Candida*, Human ecology balancing sciences, 1988

Rogers, P, *Do you feel loved by me?* , Living well publications, 1998

Rubin, J, *The maker's diet*, Thomas Nelson Inc, 1979

****

Russell Sneddon, J, *The successful treatment of Catarrh*, Thorsons publishers limited, 1948

Ryman, D, *The Aromatherapy handbook*, Century publishing Co. LTD, 1984

Sams, C, *About macrobiotics*, Thorsons publishers LTD, 1972

Sampson, A, *I wandered lonely as a cloud*, Michael O'Mara books limited, 2009

Satinover, J, *The truth behind the bible code*, Sidgwick & Jackson, 1997

Schlemmer, P, *The only planet of choice; Essential briefings from deep space*, Gateway books, 1993

Sedgbeer, S, *Complete book of beauty treatments*, Thorsons, 1994

Shapiro, D, *Your body speaks your mind*, Piatkus, 1996

Sharan, F, *Iridology*, Thornsons Publishing group, 1989

Shaw, B, *The adventures of the black girl in her search for God*, London Constable & Company Limited, 1932

Sheppard, P, *Natural Selection and heredity*, Hutchinson & Co, 1958

Simon, E, *The Reformation*, Time Inc., 1968

Simons, P, *Lecithin the cholesterol controller*, Thorsons publishing group, 1983

Speight, P, *A study course in homoeopathy*, The C.W. Daniel Company Limited, 1979

Stanway, A, *Alternative medicine*, Penguin Books LTD, 1980

Stanway, A, *A guide to Biochemic tissue salts*, Van Dyke books LTD, 1982

Stein, D, *All women are healers; A comprehensive guide to natural healing*, The Crossing Press, 1990

Stitt, P, *Fighting the food giants*, Natural Press, 1980
****

Stott, J, *God's new society,* Inter-varsity press, 1979

Symington, N, *The analytic experience,* Free association books, 1986

Tarnower, H, *The complete Scarsdale medical diet,* Bantam books, 1978

Thie, J *Touch for health,* DeVorss & Company, 1973

Thibodeau, G, *Anatomy and physiology,* Times mirror/mosby college publishing, 1987

Thomas, A, *Great books and book collectors,* Weidenfeld and Nicolson London, 1975

Thomson, J, *Fat To Flat,* Thorsons, 1995

Thurnell-Read, J, *Geopathic Stress; How earth energies affect our lives,* Element books Limited, 1995

Thurnell-Read, J, *Health Kinesiology,* Life-work potential, 2002

Tindall, B, *Anatomy & Physiology for nurses,* Cassell LTD, 1979

Tisserand, M, *Aromatherapy for women,* Thorsons Publishing Limited, 1985

Tisserand, R, *Aromatherapy for everyone,* Penguin Books, 1988

Tisserand, R, *The art of Aromatherapy,* The C.W. Daniel Company LTD, 1977

Trattler, R, *Better health through natural healing,* Thorsons pubishers Limited, 1987

Vivier, A, *Dermatology in practice,* Gower medical publishing, 1990

Von Hagens', G, *Body worlds,* Institut fur plastination, 2002

Wade, C, *Fats, Oils and Cholesterol,* Keats publishing Inc, 1973

Walker, A, *Making sense of vitamins and minerals,* Boots health and nutrition centre

Walther, D, *Applied Kinesiology,* Systems DC, 1988

****

Wangerin, W, *The book of God*, Lion publishing, 1996

Watson, L, *Supernature*, Hodder and Stoughton limited, 1973

Wesson, N, *Alternative Maternity*, Macdonald Optima, 1989

Wildwood, C, *Encyclypedia of Aromatherapy*, Bloomsbury Publishing PLC, 1996

Winston, R, *The human mind and how to make the most of it*, Transworld publishers, 2003

Winter, R, *Cosmetic Ingredients*, Crown publishers, 1989

Wunderlich, H, *The secret of Crete*, Souvenir press Ltd, 1975

A Course in Miracles, Foundation for inner peace, 1975

A Lion handbook; The world's religions, Lion publishing, 1982

Dictionary of science for everyone, Parragon Books, 1993

Elementary english grammer, HarperCollins Publishers, 1995

Lamberts:The practitioner's guide to supplements, The Reader's digest associations Limited, 2000

Lose weight and gain health, Science of life books, 1973

Revelation; Its grand climax at hand!, Watchtower bible and tract society of New York Inc., 1988

The collector's encyclopedia of Rocks and minerals, Peerage Books, 1973

The concise Oxford school dictionary, Oxford university press, 1997

The diet book, Geddes and Grosset LTD, 1996

The Lion handbook to the bible, Lion Publishing, 1973

****

Author Biography

With 30 years studying and working with the healing arts as a Holistic Therapist, Francess identifies emotional links between mind, body and spirit. In her work she explores boundaries of love and fear physiologically and emotionally and has had great success in her therapy practice with humans and animals.

After the Kinesiology technique of muscle testing was challenged by some religious individuals as a form of divination based on the scriptures saying 'those that are practicing fornication, spiritism, divination, and such things will not inherit the Kingdom of God' Fran focused her studies on the healing message of God who is Love and Light and set out to find out what made Jesus Christ the greatest healer of all time. Knowing that professional muscle testing is not divination nor is any spiritism being practiced when muscle testing is applied ethically and professionally.

Kinesiology is working with the intelligent system of the whole body based on the cell's innate sense of intelligence which goes beyond our intellectual suppositions. Fran found that pain and trauma were at the root of most ailments she worked with and realized that many problems originated with betrayals of love and trust or things classed as sin. This was certainly the case in her own life and along with mass rejection, judgements and failure to see the greater content of her work past spelling mistakes.

Having great faith in the promises of God and great faith in a God of Love who fulfills His promises to all to 'remove pain', she found pain could be removed successfully.

****

Francess conveys these understandings in her books and poetry with great appreciation for the miracle of life in the human body and demonstrates contrasting states of love, stress and fear as tangible states of being and directs all praise and glory to Our Father and Almighty Creator God of Love.

From the stars to the star fish and Genesis to Revelation her work addresses all in between to inspire love and kindness for a healing for all for happiness, joy and peace on earth.

Publications include:

Healing Poems for Positive Love (2012)   Frances Smith-Williams.

Ultimate Healing Poems – Audio CD - some available on her You Tube for free Frances Smith @ Healing Poems.
Face book Fran Smith @ Healing Poems.

Lost Loves - A poetry pamphlet to help complete the grieving process. Makes a thoughtful and lasting sympathy gift with a therapeutic application of words.

Publications include *'I Am Not a Silent Poet'*, *'London Poetry Grip'*, *'The Angry Manifesto'*, *'Penarth Times'*,*'* BBC Radio Wales', 'Cardiff   Radio', Anthologies of 'Roath Writers', 'RARA' and 'RVLF', *'Domestic Cherry' Magazine, 'Indifaring Muse',' Saravasti' Magazine, professional magazine.*

Social action projects:

Forget Me Knot campaign to raise awareness of modern day slavery.
Hidden Now Heard – Disability Wales Mental Health project, Peace poems for Armistice Day.
Multi Faith Winter Celebration and many social justice events.
'Love a Muslim Day' 3/4/18

Love's Light Exhibition 17th March to 17th May 2018
Exhibition of Photographs and Poems and launch of Parousia: Love's Light.

Francess specializes in holistic techniques for the reduction of stress, pain and PTSD with people, animals and horses for personal, bespoke sessions and is available for workshops, festivals, performance, talks and poetry readings.

Fran is qualified as: Aesthetician, numerous therapeutic massage techniques, Aromatherapist, Reflexologist, Touch for Health and Health Kinesiologist, Equine Sports Massage Therapy, counseling, nutrition, crystal skills for Kinesiologists.

www.Francess.org

You tube Frances Smith @ Healing Poems

Facebook Francess & Fran Smith @ Healing Poems

Twitter @ Healing Poems

Instagram Healing Poems.

But I am not really very social media savvy.

****

All thanks, honour, praise and glory be to God of Love and Light and who causes Love to become made whole in us for a 'Healing of All Nations' and for Heaven and Two fold Peace on Earth for all to live in paradise conditions of Love made whole in mind, body and spirit by Love conquering fear; the stress response with sinless living in accord with the laws of Love to be made whole for fulfillment of Love in us with abundance of Love, Joy, Faith, Goodness, Mildness, Kindness, Patience, Self Control not to sin for Two Fold Peace, the meaning of Jerusalem, the Holy City of Peace: Spiritual Israel: The Israel of God made real.

Amen. Ameen. Shalom. Namaste. Peace and Heaven on Earth to 'All Nations'. Amen. Ameen. Shalom. Namaste. Peace to All.

All thanks, honour, praise and glory be to God of Love and Light made whole in us for the fulfillment of Love made whole. Amen. Ameen. Shalom. Namaste. Peace to All. Thanks be to God.

'Come Lord Jesus Christ, Come'
 for fulfillment of Our Father in us.

****

The End

The end is the start of the beginning of the word endorphin
the end of the quest for heart smiles in Love
mimicked by opium posing as opiates
killing pain knowing pleasure
addictive, seductive, seducing
ending enslavement to cortisols crying for an end,
the end; the release of endorphins
the dopamine, the serotonin, the oxytocin , the anandamide
binding the blood in marriage with Love
which is always positive
the endorphin is the end
the end is the beginning of The Word; Endorphin;
His Love in our blood
The beginning of freedom;
The end is the beginning of The Promise;
His Promise
The End is the beginning

'For look I am making all things new'.

Revelation 21:5

21649016R00115

Made in the USA
Columbia, SC
24 July 2018